VICTORIAN HORSHAM

HENRY MICHELL

VICTORIAN HORSHAM

THE DIARY OF
HENRY MICHELL   1809–1874

Edited and Introduced by
KENNETH NEALE

PHILLIMORE

1975

Published by
PHILLIMORE & CO., LTD.,
Head Office; Shopwyke Hall, Chichester,
Sussex, England

ISBN 0 85033 228 1

*This book is published in
co-operation with the*
HORSHAM MUSEUM SOCIETY

Text set in 10pt. and 11/12pt. Journal
Made and printed in Great Britain by
Unwin Brothers, Ltd., Old Woking, Surrey

Sylvia Newman
Christmas 1999.

CONTENTS

PREFACE

Sussex historiography has been notably enriched by the county diarists, so the opportunity to harvest the fruits of another journal was appealing. The substance of such historically important diaries as those penned by Turner, Moore and Mantell has contributed much to our knowledge of social and local history. Thomas Turner of East Hoathly, in a provincial Pepysian style, has drawn a coarse, and in part, frivolous picture of his community in the late 18th century. The intimate record of daily life in the latter half of the previous century emerges with lively clarity from the pages of the Day Book kept by the Reverend Giles Moore, the Royalist rector of Horsted Keynes. We are similarly indebted to the Gales of Mayfield and others such as Gideon Mantell of Lewes, the eminent geologist, a man of uncommon energy and ambition. These men wrote on a considerable scale and with unusual candour and sensitivity in relation to the social nuances and domestic trifles that now cloak our knowledge of their times with otherwise unrecorded fact and an awareness that penetrates the shadow, that history on the wider canvass, can all too easily cast upon life as it was lived below the level of national affairs. Henry Michell was a humbler member of this select literary fraternity. He was not of this genre. His Victorianism precluded a preoccupation with neighbourhood trivia and the local gossip that we find so valuable in reconstituting the essence of local history. He had not much in common with his predecessors in this sense. Nor can it be said that, as a diarist, his work is of comparable dimensions or distinction. But he was actively involved, as a man of some influence, in the social and economic affairs of his community. As such he has added, in his personalised record of a busy life, an interesting and valuable chapter to the resources of local history in Horsham. What he shares in full measure with the wider company of Sussex diarists is the essential quality of authenticity. In the Michell diary we have a credible record of the world of a mid-Victorian middle-class business man in a small Sussex country town. From it we learn something about how these less eminent Victorians lived and much about how they thought in that unbelievably ephemeral age. Henry Michell was a worthy representative of the society to which he belonged. We ought to be grateful that the diary he compiled for personal and family purposes is now available, a century after his death, for public scrutiny and record.

I gladly acknowledge the assistance and encouragement I have received from the Horsham Museum Society who invited me to write this book, Mr. Bruce Michell and Commander Richard Michell who has taken a continuing interest in its production..

Kenneth Neale

West Chiltington
January 1975

INTRODUCTION

A Man of his Time

Henry Michell was born on 8 July 1809 in the green parish of Storrington, within the shadow of the silent brooding mass of Kithurst Hill. Oxen still tilled the soil and sheep bells echoed on the hillsides above the farm where he lived. The tenor of life in the Sussex farming community from which his family stemmed had its foundations in the then immutable practices and enduring qualities of rural society. His family, on a wider genealogical canvass, had had an established place in the Sussex armorial for many centuries. Nothing, it must have seemed obvious, not even the European war, then in its second decade, could seriously disturb the equilibrium of his life in that timeless environment. Yet England stood on the threshold of an unprecedented upsurge in her power and authority. The Industrial Revolution was gathering momentum and fundamental changes in English society were, historically speaking, imminent. Victorian England was to demonstrate its ability to cope with the technical and entrepreneurial aspects of that puissant age; the social and intangible dimensions of change were to prove less tractable. When Henry Michell died, in 1874, the England of his forebears had receded forever into the maw of history. His lifetime alone saw change on a scale comparable with that which had occurred throughout the whole span of the long centuries during which the Michells had cherished their Sussex lineage.

When Victoria succeeded to a throne, seriously diminished in prestige by the personal inadequacy of her Hanoverian ancestors, Henry Michell had been in Horsham but a few years. He shared in the public esteem that she attracted, which acknowledged not only the growth in national prosperity and power, but manifested a rising admiration for Creevey's[1] 'little tit of 18' who eventually became Queen Empress, restored the British monarchy and epitomised the Victorian Achievement. That was Henry Michell's world. His diary exhibits the strong and comfortable complacency that characterised the new middle-class, which was one of the more conspicuous features of the Victorian social and political scene. Within his own circles his interests, personal and intellectual, were engaged in many aspects of the Victorian century of change and progress.

The Napoleonic wars were brought to a victorious conclusion by the Allies, among whom Britain was the dynamic partner, by Wellington's decisive victory at Waterloo in 1815. Henry Michell was not quite six. Thereafter the period his life was, notwithstanding the pointless conflict in the Crimea, remarkably free from armed conflict so far as Britain was concerned. Abroad, the Franco-Prussian war, which finds its place in Henry Michell's diary towards the end of his life, and the appalling civil war in America, faint resonances of which emanate from his pages, were of profound significance. The one heralded the rise of a minatory power in Europe that was not extinguished until 1945; the other, the ascendancy of the United States in the 20th century. None of this was immediately apparent in a country obsessed with domestic issues like Parliamentary Reform, the Corn Laws, Free Trade, and the Industrial Society, all of which implicated Henry Michell in the egregious political life of Horsham in the early Victorian years.

When we come to consider Henry Michell's business activity we shall see that his success reflected, in the microcosm of a mid-Sussex market town, the burgeoning economic life of a country dedicated to *laissez faire*. New technical processes, the massive engineering of the railways, maritime supremacy in trade as well as naval armament, and the growth of a healthier population all buttressed an amazing generation of national energy led by an entrepreneurial middle class of which Henry Michell, in the humbler scale of Sussex rural life, was representative. Alongside this economic frenzy the spirit of the age was devoted to a sturdy Protestantism that finds a strong echo in the Michell diary; domestic stability and belief in the intrinsic virtues of industry, integrity and, certainly not least, property. The liberalism of the middle classes came to terms, to its own and the national advantage, with the rising political ambitions of a restless labouring population to take the place of the aristocracy and the squirearchy as their influence receded. The bulk of the English middle class was, in fact, despite legitimate anxieties about the extremism seen in Europe and at home in the ill-fated Chartist movement, broadly sympathetic to the aspirations of the proletariat which were rooted in a demand for justice and human dignity. Henry Michell was glad to associate himself with the humanity of this radical opinion and, up to a point, ready to exert himself in its cause. The middle class of Henry Michell and his peers had achieved political power as a result of the Reform Act of 1832. In retrospect that influence can be seen to have been exercised decisively, but with circumspection and without doctrinaire selfishness, in what was nevertheless an individualistic and largely materialist society. It is interesting that Henry Michell's adult life spans almost exactly the period of middle class dominance in British political life. In 1874, the year of his death, his political opponents, the Tories, heavily supported in the new working class constituencies created by the extended franchise, returned to power. From then onwards the middle class dominance of Victorian England was in decline. In its relatively brief role on the stage of British political history it had made a definitive contribution to national life and the evolution of modern society.

The vignette of a flourishing Victorian society and a nation in the ascendency must not be allowed to obscure the underlying social problems of the age. It was these that quickened the philanthropy of middle class consciences which characterised much of the Victorian social scene. Yet, surprisingly, the radical Henry Michell, in his diary at least, was not seriously concerned with or involved with the charitable activities of his class. In fact the poverty of the artisan classes and rural labourers degraded not only those unfortunate people themselves, but Victorian England itself. In the human rookeries of the towns and the wretched cottage slums of the farmlands people lived desperately near the edge of life. Public enquiries, such as Edwin Chadwick's[2] shocked and scandalised public opinion. Their findings, almost unbelieveably, were sadly all too true. In Henry Michell's youth the Sussex countryside was scarred by rioting, arson and protest as penurious labourers clamoured for half-a-crown a day. In Horsham a fracas at the parish church came near to serious violence. This was the major failure of the Victorians. The dynamism of Benthamite philosophy fired the self-made individualists who created the wealth on which future generations of Britons were nourished. But they elided their moral responsibility for the uneducated masses in their own time, who, without resources, were powerless to raise themselves from the degradation into which they had fallen. In Sussex, at one end of the social spectrum of 19th-century history was the luxuriant indolence represented by Regency Brighton; at the other were the 'Charity brats' and the poor wretches who found themselves in the 'Union'. Comfortably in the middle, was the disciplined and hard-working propertied citizenry of town and countryside which included Henry Michell.

On that somewhat sombre and enigmatic note let us turn to the Horsham in which Henry Michell lived almost the whole of the creative period of his life. When following his marriage, business took him to Horsham towards the end of 1834 it was a town of rather more than 5,000 people. The hub of the town then, as now, was the Carfax, and the main built-up area extended southwards along the Causeway to the parish church, and northwards to North Chapel, which still stands just below the modern railway station. An east-west axis lay on the line of the present East Street, and the Oxford Road, which is now called the Bishopric. Comparatively wealthy middle-class families lived in their spacious houses such as Hills Place on the outskirts of the town, on sites that have now been engulfed by modern development. The Town Hall of 1812 was the focus of public life and, situated in the heart of the town, has survived in its stony dignity to grace the northern end of the Causeway. The County Gaol,[3] an impressive building of 1779, with which Henry Michell was to be closely involved in a profitable business deal, stood in East Street roughly where the railway now crosses it. Throughout Henry Michell's life he saw the town slowly growing in size, not spectacularly, but, after the arrival of the railway from Three Bridges in 1848, purposefully. The rail link via Warnham from Dorking was not completed until 1867. By 1874 Horsham's population was about 8,000, a rate of growth over the 40 years that Henry Michell lived in the town, that by Victorian standards was no more than average for a country town of the status of Horsham.

It is a salutary thought that when the coming of the railway marked the advent of a modern industrial society, Horsham had but a few years previously witnessed the last vestiges of medieval practices, which unfortunately escaped the notice of Henry Michell's diary though not of the contemporary press. In 1844 some 3,000 people had flocked to the last public execution in the town which had lost its Assize status to Lewes in 1830. In the same year at least one woman was said to have been offered for sale, publicly in the Carfax, by an unappreciative, or indigent, husband. Such squalid eipsodes were not the only blemishes on the public life of the town.

Horsham had been a notorious pocket borough, and it
was not until the Reform Act of 1832 that the era of
corruption and political domination by the Irwins and
the Dukes of Norfolk was brought to an end. The bizarre
story of iniquity and disorder was told, graphically and
with authority, in William Albery's compendious parliamentary history of Horsham. Henry Michell, who to his
credit, appears to have disapproved strongly of these
excesses, played a notable part in the mid-century elections in the town. Not until the Ballot Act of 1872
conferred a respectable privacy on the electoral process
was Horsham altogether freed from the malpractice and
vicissitudes of the so-called 'open' elections.

If its parliamentary life was disreputable, Horsham's
local administration was hardly better, though it is only
fair to say that this was fairly general at municipal level
in Victorian England before the reforms. Apathy and
downright neglect characterised the management of
local affairs which were in the hands of self-centred
and reactionary men. The public utilities, though the first
gas lighting had reached the town by 1836, and cultural
institutions were, from lack of public support, never
effectively developed until towards the end of the 19th
century. Yet, when it was not arranging its parliamentary
representation or minding its municipal business, Horsham
was a pleasant busy little market town in which the
urbanities of middle class society harmonised with the
material satisfactions of a trading and working class
community that enjoyed, by virtue of the town's economic validity, a measure of immunity from the recurrent
depressions that impoverished the agricultural population
in the rural parishes.

Horsham's economy was based on a corpus of craftsmen
and tradesmen, whose little businesses complemented the
larger enterprises of the wealthier men of commerce like
Henry Michell, and the local markets. In 1852 a new
cattle market had been established in the Bishopric. A
corn market flourished in Swan Alley until 1862 after

which a new Corn Exchange and Market in West Street,
opened in 1868, continued to attract the mid-Sussex
farmers and a variety of traders who lent vitality to the
business life of the town. Among the minor industries
carried on in the town, aside from the essential country
trades such as blacksmithing and wheelwrighting, were
rope-making, basket-making, broom manufacture, saddlery,
shoe- and glove-making, and a clay pipe factory. The
traders included such as Pickett the ironmonger, Boyne
the draper, Chambers the butcher, and Knight the grocer.
Necessary in a market town, with a regular visiting population, were the numerous inns, foremost among which
were the *King's Head,* the *Crown* and the *Swan.* The
centre of the town, and East Street particularly, did not
look all that different from its appearance just before
the recent redevelopment. The layout and rooflines
were broadly the same; there was a lot more weather-
boarding, and shop fronts had a homely domestic air.
And, just as today's roads are frequently thronged with
cars so the coaches and the horse-drawn vehicles of the
traders and village carriers, such as James Norris of West
Chiltington, who drove into Horsham once a week with
farm produce, crowded the narrow streets of the town.
On market days all was hustle in this lively little wealden
metropolis. It all had an air of purpose; that of earning
its living. Henry Michell was good at that, too, and must
have found Horsham highly compatible with his own
ambitions, if not always with his own high moral tone.

We have but glanced, superficially, at the general picture
of Victorian England, and at life in Horsham in the age
in which Henry Michell lived there. Now this introduction
must focus on the diarist himself. Later, in the connecting
narrative of this presentation of his diary, I shall elaborate
on those aspects that bear most directly on his life. Here,
it will be convenient to consider briefly the motivation
of the writer and the reality of his life and diary. I shall
explain, too, how it has been adapted for the purpose
of this book.

I have sought to present Henry Michell as a man in
harmony with the context of his life. In the diary we
find him involved in the things that mattered most to
the Victorian middle class. Family life, a thrusting
business, travel, public life, and moralising, all emerge
as part of the pattern of this Horsham worthy's life. We
may regret that, as is often the case with documents of
this kind, the local orientation of the diary is, in many
important aspects, deficient. Similarly, allowances have
to be made for the fact that it was written, presumably,
from multifarious notes and records, towards the end of
the author's life, between 1871 and 1874. It thus lacks
the spontaneity and pristine authenticity of contemporary recording. We may, I think, generally accept
the factual account of his family life and business
activity. But, it would be prudent to assume that the
political material has, to some extent at least, benefited
from the hindsight that retrospection confers. This,
although it diminishes the historical validity of the diary,
is not necessarily a serious weakness. We may still appre-
ciate the matters that most concerned the writer, and
certainly his considered views emerge with a clarity that
defies contradiction. A century after his death we can
know with confidence what Henry Michell believed
and the philosophy that governed his views and conduct
in private and public life.

That much was clear from a first reading. The problem
was to decide how to select and organise the material
for a public that will require some evaluation of the
contents of the diary, as well as a readable and coherent
presentation of what might otherwise be turgid and
confusing. The methodology I have adopted is therefore
designed to satisfy these criteria. It will be seen that the
layout of the diary falls broadly into three parts. These
cover Henry Michell's life in its domestic, business and
public aspects. To facilitate this and sustain the chrono-
logy it has been necessary to re-arrange some sections
of the diary. I also found it desirable to present the

domestic section on a different basis since, as it contained long and repetitive passages describing foreign tours not relevant to the general context of the book, it would not bear reproduction at any considerable length. This, I think will be helpful to the reader in concentrating what would otherwise be much divergent and uncoordinated material.

It was to be expected that in parts the diary would be somewhat pedestrian and repetitive and thus unsuitable for publication in its original form. In parts, therefore, the editing has been severe. I hope the diary and the image of Henry Michell as a representative Victorian middle-class citizen of Horsham has benefited thereby. In the main the diary, supported by the narrative, must speak for itself although I have, in the concluding chapter, ventured to assess Henry Michell as a man with an identifiable role in the life of a mid-Sussex market town in Victoria's England.

I thought it right not to edit the syntax, orthography and punctuation in the text of the diary which is printed as Henry Michell wrote it.

I

VICTORIAN FAMILY MAN
'Calm Retrospection'

'I can very well imagine that some years hence, this book may fall into the hands of some member of my family who may very well ask "who was Henry Michell of Grandford House?" '4

So Henry Michell introduced his diary. He can hardly have imagined that a Horsham Museum Society, not founded until 1893, would aspire, not merely to know who he was, but to publish the diary as a contribution to Horsham history 100 years after his death. Doubtless, had that been so he would have contrived, to our delight, to have recorded more of the affairs of the town. As it is, the orientation of the diary is towards the natural curiosity that his family might be expected to exhibit about his personal and business life. The diary continues:

Well, for the information of such an one, I will state as briefly as possible who I am, and whence I came, and to do this it may be necessary to say something of my ancestors who lived for 200 years, I have been informed, at Hermongers in the parish of Rudgwick, certain it is that my Father was born there on the   of Augt 1780, his Father Edward Michell was born there also and there he died of smallpox in 1782 and was buried on the east side of Rudgwick church, where a stone now marks his grave, he left 2 children very young, my Father and Mary Michell (married to Edward Eager of Graffham) it seems there was only one son for several generations, as my great grandfather, John Michell was married twice and left two families as follows—. First family Sarah (Mrs Mills) Mary (Mrs Trower) Jane (Mrs Butt)

Second family, Leah (Mrs Mann of Tismans), Anne (Mrs Ireland of Garlands) and one son Edward, my Grandfather. Mrs Trower became a widow and then married Mr Napper, who served the office of Sheriff for Sussex, she had one son Edward, the Father of the late Edward Napper and Grandfather of the present John Napper of Ifold House near Petworth.

My Father married Mary Turner of Chancton and had twelve children viz: Edward, John, Henry, George, Jane and Matilda, Alfred and Mark, Ellen, Luke, Matthew and Mary, we all lived to grow up and once we all met around my Father's table at the Brewery, Steyning—and never but once.

About the year 1805 my Father sold Hermongers to Lord Egremont and bought Kithurst and Cootham farms in the Parish of Storrington where seven of us were born, myself among the rest on the 8th of July 1809, but farming from one cause or other was a very bad business for several years after the conclusion of the great war at the Battle of Waterloo in 1815 June 18—, and my Father embraced the opportunity of taking a Brewery at Steyning whither we all removed on the 30th day of September 1822.

The means for education at this time were not so liberal as they are now. I was sent for 2 or 3 years to the village school at Storrington kept by a man named Lefford and tho by no means a scholar in a classical sense, he possessed a good stock of sound common sense and was a truly good Christian man, and his wife was a very excellent woman and they were both much beloved by all their little pupils, and I lived to know they were much respected by all their neighbours, I feel it is my duty as well as privilege to pay this passing tribute of respect to their memory.

In 1816 I was sent to a proprietory school at Pulboro conducted by Mr W Billinghurst, and a most excellent school it was. I believe I may say I made good progress in my studies and was on excellent terms with my Tutors and school fellows and was as happy as any boy can expect to be at school but unfortunately Mr Billingshurst's abilities were not appreciated in the neighbourhood sufficiently to make it worth his while to remain at Pulboro, and in 1819 he left and went to Hitchin in Hertfordshire where he shortly after died. He was succeeded at Pulboro by a Mr Saunders of whom the less said the better, he staid but a little while and was succeeded in 1821 by a Mr Gandell who was a first rate English and French master. I staid with him till I left school in 1824 being now in my fifteenth year.

I had a great inclination for commercial business and it suited my Father's wishes that I should go into the Brewery where I laboured early and late until the year 1833 when to my great joy and as it has subsequently proved to my great advantage, Mr Luke Upperton of Thakeham proposed to my Father that I should take the management of their branch bank at Steyning. I entered upon my duties on the first of January 1833 and I found the system of book keeping as there adopted proved how little I knew of book keeping before, and I discerned at once how essential to success in life a thorough knowledge of it is, experience in life has convinced me how very little it is understood, and that a very large number of those who pass through our bankruptcy courts have been compelled to do so from their ignorance of it. I had occasion to attend the Bankruptcy Court in Basing Hall Street in the matter of James Fairs of Southwater about the year 1850 and the commissioner said that a very large majority of cases that came before him arose entirely from ignorance of Book keeping. The whole business connected with the Bank suited my views and ideas to a tittle and I thoroughly enjoyed it, but, alas like every thing appertaining to what old Frances Moore[5] calls 'Mundane affairs' it was of very short duration for it so happened that in June 1830 a young lass came to pay a visit to our House with whom I fell in love at first sight, for it was no other than my dear wife[6] and after a courtship of over 4 years we thought, at least I did, that it was time to get married, so I left the Bank and Steyning and came here on the 3rd of October 1834 (we were married at Binsted Church Sept 23) and on the first of January 1835 entered on these premises as successor to William Allen in the Brewing business.

I very soon found the difference between looking forward to having a business of my own and the reality, Oh with what fear and trembling my feelings alternated between hope and despair, sometimes I thought I was going to make a fortune in a hurry and then things looked adverse and I fancied nothing but ruin stared us in the face, but my dear wife was always a safe resort in times of trouble and we often took sweet counsel together and having resolved to do that which we believed to be right and committing ourselves and our affairs into the hands of our heavenly Father we went on our way with confidence as to the future, I made very slow progress however owing to very great competition in the trade and the Barley harvest was very indifferent for several consecutive years from 1837 to 1841 inclusive.

In 1839, December 21, our home was brightened up by the arrival in the flesh of a very dear little girl, she was baptized Fanny Matilda, the former after her maternal grandmother and the latter name after my sister (Mrs Ellis).

As my lease of these premises would terminate on the 31st of December 1841 and I could come to no reasonable terms with Mr Allen for a renewal thereof I availed myself of the opportunity which offered to take the premises belonging to the Shelley family[7] called New Buildings and where the Rawlinson family had for meny years carried on the Brewing business, whither we removed on the 25th March 1841 and here we remained (it is now, and for many years has been called the West Street Brewery) until the 31st of May in this present year 1870, when we returned to these premises.

Later in life, in 1870 the year of Forster's education Act, and perhaps prompted by that, Henry Michell recorded with pride, and approval of the improvements that had taken place since his schooldays:

In the course of my education at Pulborough School under Mr. Billinghurst I gained a prize at Midsummer 1818, which, though nothing to boast of in a scholastic sense, I am rather proud of for the encomium which my master wrote when inscribing my name on the fly leaf, and which is as follows:

Master H. Michell
Prize
for Writing and for obtaining the love of
all his Companions as well as his Teachers.
Midsummer 1818.

The Book itself was called the 'Stories of Old Daniel', and a very miserable set of stories they were. When I think of the usefulness and variety of books provided for all classes now, as compared with those days, it is impossible to over-rate the advantages of the present time.

Family life in Horsham was happy for the Michells but they did not at once find their local social round altogether satisfactory. Children came—Fanny Malilda in 1839 and Henry in 1843—and, ever great travellers, they sustained their old friendships with an assiduity both remarkable and commendable:

> When we first came to Horsham we visited several families, but, there was such a rage for cardplaying and other things which did not at all agree with our tastes that a sort of mutual coolness accrued between us which finally left us all but completely isolated; nevertheless we had occasionally some old friends to stay with us, among others was Eliza Newland from Goring, she was indeed a dear friend of my wife's and a sincere Christian I believe; she died as several of her family did of consumption about 1840 (at Worthing).
>
> In the spring of 1836 my dear wife was confined of a still-born female child which was a very great disappointment to us both, in 1839 our daughter (now Mrs Cowan) was born, as before stated December 21st.
>
> 1840. Nothing particular occurred to us this year till towards the end when we began preparing for our removal to the premises now used as the West Street Brewery.
>
> 1841. We began this year with busy preparations for the same which we completed, and entered upon our new home on the 25th of March and I must say we enjoyed the change very much, the premises altogether being so very preferable to these from a business point of view, and as a home as well.
>
> 1842. Nothing particular occurred to us this year, we were both of us blessed with pretty good health and our dear little girl grew, if not in wisdom and stature, at least very much in favour with Papa and Mama.
>
> 1843. This year on the 19th of May our Son was born and a very weakly specimen of humanity he was, he was baptized at Horsham old church in the July following my wife's brother Edward Ellis and Miss Pinnock acting as sponsors. At this time we were intimate with Mrs Pinnock and her daughter and also with Mr and Mrs Pennyfeather of the London and County Bank here and very nice friends they proved to be. We may reckon Miss Pinnock still one of our friends; her mother has long since paid the debt of nature. The Pennyfeathers removed to Huntingdon about 1844 and then to Romford a few years later when Mr Pennyfeather died.
>
> A young man named Francis Teale who had lived with us as a pupil in the business left us, he had been with us two years and I would never take another.

In 1844, the Michells found their way to Dover and thence by sea to Ramsgate and the Thames for an annual visit that in previous years had taken them to Suffolk, Hastings, Brighton, Portsmouth, and Somerset, despite the difficulties of travel, for as he says:

> It must be borne in mind there were very few railways in those days and a 90 mile ride outside a stage coach was no very trifling matter and particularly for my dear wife.

But there were, apart from the pleasures of seeing friends and relatives, compensations especially for one, such as Henry Michell, whose lively interest in places and events is apparent from the detailed entries in his diary. At Clifton, near Bristol:

> we put up at an Hotel almost close to the pier of the contemplated Suspension bridge[8] (since completed); we enjoyed the scenery here very much being so different to anything we had ever seen before; the Great Briton[9] was being constructed in the Docks at Bristol; the largest ship then known, and built entirely of iron and looked upon as almost one of the wonders of the World.

He had an eye for scenery too:

> I believe we have by this time (1870) been in nearly every county in England; 3 times into Wales and once into Scotland, but nowhere in England have we ever seen scenery more beautiful than the counties of Surrey and Sussex, excepting of course the Lake scenery of Westmorland, Cumberland etc.

Each year of the diary demonstrates Michell's insatiable appetite for travel. Business took him to East Anglia where he admired the castle and cathedral at Norwich, although he was not generally impressed with 'a very irregular and badly paved city'. Railway trips, steamboat journeys along the south coast, coach travel to the North Downs and a visit *en famille* to the London Zoo all figured in the annual ritual of leisure travel which was such a feature of middle-class family life at the time.

An echo of the hazards of life in 19th-century England was sounded in 1847 when Henry Michell noted:

> Our children now went to the Miss Evershed's school in the Bishopric and I believe it was this year that the smallpox broke out in the school and both of them failed with it but slightly as they had previously been vaccinated.[10]

The 25th May 1848 was a red-letter day in the log of the Michell peregrinations:

> we drove a dear little pony we then possessed called, Nanny, to the Worthing station and there took the rail which was only just opened to Portsmouth to witness one of the grandest sights I should think ever seen in the opening of the new Basin for the construction and repairs of the steam shipping of England's Navy. We hired a boat at the Hard and went on board a merchant ship when the Queen Victoria came up in her yacht from Cowes and stopped close to us to take the Duke of Wellington on board and so we saw the meeting of the old Duke and Queen and very cordial it seemed to be. The roar of cannons and the playing of the numerous bands of music was really deafening. We left Portsmouth at 7 p.m. and reached home again at 11, highly delighted with our day excursion.

The family had been filled with 'awe and admiration' on their visit to Stonehenge in 1850 and their trips to the Isle of Wight always offered the possibility of a glimpse of the Queen's official visitors. There were, too, excursions to London, Brighton, and the other south coast resorts. But it was the Great Exhibition of 1851, to which we shall come, and an expedition to North Wales that Henry Michell saw as the 'grand tour compared with which all our previous travels were cast into the shade'. When they were old enough and schooling allowed, the children accompanied their parents on their travels. Both, in the fashion of the Victorian middle class were at boarding school. Fanny was at Miss Summers' at Dorking, and Harry, after attending the Grammar School at Steyning was sent to Queenwood College near Stockwell in

Hampshire where the principals were 'just the right sort of people to bring boys up, a little by the rules of commonsense'. Harry they could leave 'in very good spirits', but the partings with Fanny were 'wretched . . . several times a year'. However, Victorian family discipline was satisfied and certainly the family ties seem to have been strengthened by these absences, since the children, throughout their lives, enjoyed the affection and generosity of the parents to the full. The recurring disability of gout, although distressing, and indeed almost conventional for a Victorian gentleman, was never allowed to frustrate Henry Michell's programme of travel. In 1858 we find them enjoying the scenic delights of the Lake District returning to Horsham 'highly gratified with our Tour, the total cost of which was £52:18:4. which we considered very moderate as we travelled first class by rail always, a pair of horses by road and always put up at first class hotels'. Harry was 'packed off to Queenswood' to continue his course in commonsense and self-reliance! The Michells, with the development of the railways which provided frequent services from Horsham, continued to look further afield for their recreation. Returning to North Wales in 1859 they walked, rode and drove in the mountains to the intense satisfaction of the family instincts for tourism; it was again considered all good value. Though gout intervened again in the following spring, by the summer of 1860 the family were off to Derbyshire and the stately homes of Haddon Hall and Chatsworth about which Henry Michell was 'all but dumb. Its grandeur surpasses any description I can give'. Indefatiguable, they visited the caves and Warwick Castle, but still found time for church on Sunday morning and the energy for a further visit to Brighton before settling down for the winter and the 'ordinary quietude' of their comfortable domestic life.

The development of travel and recreation for other than the wealthy classes, for whom Paris and the Italian tour had long been a social and cultural necessity, was a

conspicuous feature of Victorian life. The engineers, Tel-
ford, McAdam, Rennie, and Stephenson, with their roads,
bridges and railways, laid the foundation for the almost
ritualistic addiction of the English to the annual holiday.
For the rising artisan classes this was symbolised by the
steam-boats that took them to Southend, Margate and
Ramsgate. The comfortable self-conscious lower middle
classes found solace at Folkestone, Brighton and Bognor.
Later it was Clacton for the masses; Worthing for the
genteel. It was the age of the bandstand, the bathing-
machine, the pier, and the guide-book all evocatively
depicted in the literature and art of the period which
exactly captured the flavour of this ingredient in the
expanding social life of the people. Economic progress
had enabled them to afford it; the facilities for travel
had been provided by Victorian enterprise and ambition.
By the early 1840s the railways had consolidated their
primary role in communications. Queen Victoria had
made her first journey on the permanent way and was
'quite charmed by it'.

The Ruskins[11] lent a cultural dimension to travel which
was taken up with characteristic enthusiasm by Victorian
middle-class worthies such as Henry Michell, who, like
the modern American tourist, had an insatiable desire
to know and to see. Europe represented the zenith of the
holiday adventure and was characterised by complicated
arrangements, exhausting local tours and a spirit of
romance and sentimentality that was never to be recap-
tured in the more sophisticated climate of our time.
The Michells participated to the full and France, the
Rhine tour and Switzerland, then 'the new playground
of Europe', as Mona Wilson[12] has called it. All figured
in the Michell itineraries which enjoy a generous propor-
tion of our subject's diary.

Thus the Michells indulged in the new 'holiday game'
made possible by rising affluence and the growth of
communications. The journeys I have so far mentioned
were but the prelude to more ambitious excursions.

The year 1861 saw the family off to Scotland and the Highlands when Henry Michell had satisfied himself that 'the business could run alone for about 2 or 3 weeks'. Inverness, the Caledonian Canal, Edinburgh, Glasgow, and the Clyde; all were taken in their stride. For this extensive tour, £92 6s. 6d. was 'entered in the books'. The year 1863 was begun with 'anticipation of more than normal pleasure' as an European tour was planned. However, first, towards the end of 1862, Henry Michell re-traced the footsteps of his childhood:

> On 26th. of August we carried out a long talked of visit to Kithurst in the Parish of Storrington. Miss Penwick was staying with us. We hired an open carriage here and pair of horses and reached Storrington about 12 o'clock, put up at the old Inn, the White Horse, and had lunch and ordered dinner. We then started off and went up the Church street to the foot of Chantry down, which we ascended and then walked along the crest of the hill to Parham post. We then returned and descended by the old chalk pit and lime kilns to Kithurst house and thence by the pond out to the common and back to the Inn just in time for dinner. Mrs. Lee had provided us with a leg of most excellent mutton, and an apple pudding with most delicious cream, to all of which I need hardly say we did most ample justice: we were one and all very tired and hungry. I had not been over this same ground on which I had spent my childhood and early years (up to 14) for more than 20 years, and how well I remembered the magnificent view from the highest point of Kithurst down.[13] I believe it is the highest ground west of Chanctonbury ring, and every object seemed to bring up reminisences of years long, long gone by. My Father sold the Kithurst estate to the Honble. Robert Curzon about 1830, and consequently not much change had taken place upon it except for the worse. All the fences and gates were all down or very bad, and the buildings much out of repair: in fact it looked as I believe all property must, or is very likely to look, which is owned by a bankrupt and occupied by a rogue.

The European adventure began on a wet and windy day, 20 May 1863:

> As we left home people were going off to the Derby at Epsom, all in the rain. Some of them supposed we had

taken leave of our senses and were going there too, but when
I told them we were off for a tour in Switzerland they were
dumbfounded and stared with astonishment.

The Michells' aversion to gambling, whether with cards
or on the turf, was more than matched by their appetite
for the sights of Europe. Calais, Brussels, Cologne, and by
steamer up the Rhine en route to Basle, provided a
crowded itinerary for their first few days on the continent.
But, unfortunately, the tour was curtailed by Mrs. Michell's
illness and so they turned homewards via Berne, Geneva,
and Paris. Henry Michell's copious notes nevertheless
testify to the enthusiasm and interest which their European adventure aroused. Mrs. Michell's illness was found
to be smallpox and the whole family was infected:

> Mrs. Michell's illness proved to be smallpox, but Dr. Demi
> would not let us know this till just before we left. Whether
> he had told Mr. Kraft of it or not, we never knew. If he did,
> it was fortunate for us we were not consigned to some pest
> house as prisoners. As to how she came by it, it is quite
> clear she must have had it before we left England, as she was
> very unwell only the third day after, and she has no doubt
> she took it from some loathsome looking children laying
> by the roadside at Springfield (about a week before we left
> home) which she passed on her way on foot to Wimblehurst,
> as she remarked at the time they smelled quite offensively.
> Harry left us to go on to Chamounix for Geneva and to meet
> us there on Saturday, June 6. We left Berne accordingly.
> Mrs. Michell bore the journey quite as well as we could have
> expected. We put up at the Hotel Des Bergue but Harry did
> not join us till the next morning, Sunday the 7th. He had
> been obliged to travel nearly all night and he was completely
> done up the next day. He did not get any better, and dear
> Fanny and myself felt very unwell, but I felt sure it could
> not be the smallpox as I had had it when a child by inocula-
> tion by Dr. Dennett at Storrington, and we knew our children
> had had it quite decidedly in 1847 by infection from Miss
> Evershed's school. However, we were so weak and queer I
> insisted on sending for medical aid, and we were attended
> by a Dr. Metcalf, an Englishman. He assured us we were all
> suffering from that disease, but that the crises was past, and
> as we had it very lightly there was no fear of our giving

infection to any one. We were very willing to believe this, and it was a great comfort to us at the time, but I have often thought since it was wrong of us to travel.

They were glad to reach 'dear old England again', and Horsham on 15 June 1863, after nearly a month away; undeterred and grateful:

> Our tour cost us about £120, and the result was to convince us of the pleasures and advantages to be derived from time and money spent in such manner and we resolved to repeat it the very first favourable opportunity . . . Altogether this seemed a very momentous year with us. We had accomplished our first foreign tour and come safely through what might have been a very serious event to us, and a calm retrospection of it demands our sincere thanks to Almighty God for his great mercies to all of us.

The next year, 1864, saw Fanny's marriage to a Mr. T. W. Cowan, a trip to Lands End and the West Country, severe gout and a visit to Crystal Palace to see Garibaldi, the 'Hero of Italian Unity, the sworn foe of despotism, and priestcraft', as Henry Michell described him.

Thoughts turned again to Europe in 1865. The diarist dwells eagerly and nostalgically on his sojourns in Switzerland which he clearly regarded as providing some of the highlights of his personal life:

> I cannot conclude my narrative of this tour without saying that it was altogether a source of heartfelt and unbounded satisfaction. If I look back to the days of my boyhood, early manhood, or even middle age, I always consider the advantages of travelling in foreign countries as blessings reserved for something like a different order of beings to ourselves, but prosperity at home, and facility of travelling by rail and steamboat abroad, opened my eyes to the fact that even we might partake of them; most thankful am I that we were permitted to do so, as the language, manners and customs of the people, the views, lakes and mountain scenery, of a continental country as compared with our Island home creates in one's mind a class of ideas, and affords a never-ending source for contemplation. The cost of this tour, which I like to insert for the guidance of others was £140.

The rich flavour of the continental tour was reflected in the diary the following year when the Michells, in a somewhat blasé mood:

> resolved upon leading a very quiet life this year, as we looked now upon such little excursions as to Brighton, Beckenham, and even in Wales, as very small affairs and hardly to be called tours at all.

Truly, the family horizons had enlarged with the business, and in harmony with the developing pattern of Victorian middle-class life. Eighteen hundred and sixty-eight took them yet again to the continent, this time to France, which, although it impressed them did not evoke the uncritical admiration reserved for Switzerland and 'dear old Berne'. The same year the Michells started to rebuild their Horsham home:

> We planted some trees as soon as possible to save one year and we then completely gutted the house, stripped all the old stone healing off the roof and raised it with attic floors and partitions by means of screws about 3 feet which enabled us to set all the rooms out a good height, the only actual additions we made were enlarging the cellars, the stairs and the porch which enabled us to complete all the arrangements according to my own plan, as I hold a nice entrance hall and a commodius stairs to be the greatest desiderata in house architecture. We left nothing of the old house but the roof etc. as before described, and the outer walls. We got it all healed[14] in and barricaded the windows before winter set in.
> We pushed our operations on vigorously, and by the end of the year it was completed, excepting the papering, painting, etc. One thing I must mention here, that is the name of this house, and why we had it called 'Grandford House'. After our removal from here in 1841 these premises were turned into a Hotel called the 'Richmond Hotel'. When I bought it by auction in 1853 I immediately did away with it and let it as a private house, and it was called Richmond house, a name I had no affection for, and so I looked into the deeds and found that it formerly formed part of a property of which the meadow adjoining the garden was also a part and was called Grandfords, so we resolved upon adopting this name.

1870. With the beginning of this year we entered earnestly
into the business of finishing and furnishing this house with
a view to moving into it quite by the beginning of Summer.
We went to Beckenham in February, and thence to London
several times to buy furniture etc. At the end of March we
went to stay with our friends, the Morts, for 3 or 4 days,
from whence we did a good deal of shopping. We also went
to Brighton and made considerable purchases of Ironmongery
and Upholstery. The superintendence of the decorations
and finishing of the papering, painting etc. and receiving and
arranging the furniture and removing some from the West
Street Brewery gave us all pretty full occupation for some
time. At last we made up our minds that we would fix the
first of June as the day on which we proposed to ourselves
to wake up in the morning and find ourselves in our new
abode, and I hope and trust we are all thankful that we were
permitted to realize our desires but the effect of the change
upon myself I can hardly describe. I had, I may say, been fully
engaged in business from boyhood and to feel that I was even
only partly relieved from its obligations was an inexpressible
relief, and I am looking forward to a further relaxation as I
hope soon to give it all up to my son in whom it gives me great
pleasure to say I have full confidence. Oh, what a glorious
happy thing to be able to say this; surely my dear wife and
myself may say, though it may be with all humility, that we
did endeavour to fulfil the proverb of Solomon 'To train up
a child in the way he should go, etc.'

I think this is the proper place to give a little account of the
cost of our new home. The old house, including the Literary
institution and all the premises was rated in my books under
the head of real property at £2000. I gave Mr. George Holmes
£525, and we laid out altogether on the house and gardens
and outbuildings about £3000, making a total of £5525, of
which I considered £1525 as sunk, and charged it to the Profit
and Loss account accordingly, and therefore leaving the house
now known as Grandford house with the meadow (for which
I gave £525 to Mr. Holmes as before mentioned) and the
whole of the premises including the Literary institution and
all the furniture at a cost as standing in the books of £4000.

It was time too, for this Horsham worthy, now a man of
substance, to be recorded on canvass. So in 1869:

We were looking forward at the beginning of this year to
being busy enough with our house without much thinking

about touring, but one little incident I must here mention. My dear wife and family were very desirous I should have my portrait painted and as there happened to be a Mr. Martin located here for a short time, who was reputed a good artist in this way, I invoked his services and hence my portrait, which some say is admirable and some it is not good, but who are right and who are wrong it is not for me to say.

Eighteen hundred and sixty-nine was a year of family events, happy and sad:

I must not close these memos of 1869 without recording the most joyful event of a domestic character that has happened to us for some time, in the birth of a dear little grandson. Mrs. Cowan was confined at Ryde house, Beckenham, on the 15th. of August. Of course we went to see our daughter and the little stranger in about 2 months, and we pronounced him as the very prettiest and best little baby we had ever seen without prejudice to other people's grandchildren notwithstanding. Truly I begin to realize what I have read of the great statesman, Count Bismark, when he said that 'as we grow in years old friends drop off on all sides of us, we get too old to form new friendships and if we have no grandchildren we seem to have no connecting link with the surviving human family'. About Xmas Mrs. Cowan and her dear Baby came to stay a few weeks with us, which I need hardly say we very much enjoyed. My Mother died on the 22nd. day of November in one of the new houses at the back of Church Street, Steyning, aged 86.

Henry Michell tried his hand, too, with a gun, though he never appears to have relished shooting as a good country bourgeois should!

I gave up shooting this year: I had done but very little at it for a year or two. I never liked shooting much in anticipation. I believe it was because I could not very well spare the time, and I was so often troubled with gout and short breathing I found it hard work, but still, when I was regularly at it I enjoyed it very much, and though not a dead shot, I performed very well at times and could bear as much fatigue as most people up to the time before narrated. When I used Stakers farm, I shot over this land, and Muggaridge's, and several small farms, altogether nearly 400 acres, embracing some most magnificent views of the Weald and South downs. I can call to mind many delightful days spent there, such, I believe, as fashionable sportsmen know not of. I hate the batteau system, with lots of beaters driving a lot of tame birds into a corner: one may as well almost go into the Farm yard and shoot the fowles. I used to like going out by myself and a good faithful dog to find my game, and to be satisfied with a moderate bag. At the beginning of the season I liked a companion or two very well. So much for my shooting career, but I will not close this subject without saying, for the guidance of those who may choose to listen to me, that when I began business I did not begin shooting. I plodded on 16 years before I took out a sporting license; in plain words I may say I got some money to spend before I began spending. I now see it is too often the case for young men to begin business and sporting simultaneously, and often with what result deponent saith not.

The shadows of old age approached:

1872 was ushered in as usual by a merry peal from the Church bells. I was awake and heard them, and I thought in my own mind, who of all those who might be listening to them, as well as myself, would be taken to their final account before the new year had run out. Death has certainly reaped a plentiful harvest in this Town within the last six or seven years. When I look around on the congregation in our old Church I see hardly any left of all those we knew as the heads of households when we first came to Horsham. Well, all this should remind us how frail is man, and of the necessity of each one of us being prepared when our time may come.

I continued very unwell all the Spring and could not venture to church before the beginning of May, having been absent 6 months a thing that had never occurred to me before.

Henry Michell's son's wedding was a matter for a great family celebration. It was also commemorated in the business with typical Victorian patronage:

While on this subject, I must say a little of what took place at home. It would have been unkind, to say the least of it, to have passed over all our employees without some little memento of our son's marriage, and after consulting with my Wife and Son, we resolved upon giving to everyone in our employ a new sovereign neatly enclosed in a note to each and written with my own hand, of which the following is an exact copy:

> *Please to accept this sovereign for the benefit of yourself*
> *and family, as a gift on the marriage of my Son this day, and*
> *as a token of good will between masters and men.*
>   *Henry Michell, May 22, 1872.*

The total number to whom this gift was made was 44, to
the female domestics and boys also a small present was made,
and I think I ought not to omit to mention that a bottle of
champagne was also given to each man. Altogether I believe we
may say we gave great satisfaction to them all and they testified to their good will and affection for the new married
couple by uniting to make them a very handsome present at a
cost of something like £20. The total cost of gifts to the men
as stated above was £43. 12. 6.

I also thought that some little present should be made to
each of our Trade customers, more of course as a compliment
than any consideration of value, and with that view I wrote a
note to each, of which the following is a copy:

> *'Sir. I am pleased to inform you that my son is to be*
> *married this day and I beg your acceptance of the small*
> *gratuity of 10/- to celebrate the happy event, and which I*
> *hope you will spend in any way most agreeable to yourself.*
> *The amount will be allowed in next settlement. Yours truly,*
> *Henry Michell. May 22, 1872.*

This note was sent to each person on the 21st. so that
they received it on the wedding day. There were 80 of them
and the total cost was £40.

Eighteen hundred and seventy-four opened well enough,
but Henry Michell died, peacefully in his devoted son's
presence, on 25th October 1874:

All through the last winter we had no severe weather at
all. The Ice on Warnham mill pond was sufficiently strong
to bear skating upon it for 2 or 3 days only; after that we had
mild weather for the season up to the end of April, when it
set in very cold and dry right up to midsummer, though there
were occasional showers, just enough to make the grass grow,
but there was not a great crop of Hay, and some of it was
spoiled in the making. It has proved an excellent season for
the corn crop, which I believe is the best we have had at
Shiprods ever since we have had the Farm. We began reaping
on the 29th. of July, and we have now finished, excepting a
few oats, including second cut hay and all. The weather

was a little showery up to Thursday eve, the 13th. since which we had glorious sunshine and the Harvest is nearly completed all over the country. The swifts took their departure on Friday, the 21st. of this month. It was a brilliant, sunny day, but there was rather a keen wind from the north which I believe induced them to leave, as there were a great many of them rushing and screaming up and down our gateway in the morning, but in the evening there was not one to be seen, but there seems one solitary bird left behind which I have seen both yesterday and today.

II

MAN OF BUSINESS
'Upon the whole . . . very satisfactory'

The quotation that provides the sub-title to this chapter
would, I think, serve more than adequately for Henry
Michell's personal life in all its aspects. In his business
affairs it is perhaps an understatement, for that they were
very successful will be obvious from that part of the diary,
which I have decided to reproduce with only a few minor
editorial deletions dictated by form and presentation.

Henry Michell's addiction to business discipline and the
exacting standards that he set are evident from the opening
passages of this section of the diary. The world of state
intervention, collective bargaining and fiscal manipulation
as an instrument of government was virtually unknown
to him, although all these factors of modern economic
life were beginning to emerge. His concern was with hard
work, prudent investment, cost accounting and enterprise. These indeed were the essential ingredients of
business success in a Victorian England as yet untram-
melled by the complicated and inhibiting notions of
social relevance, the arts and artifices of personnel
management and public accountability. He made the
most of his opportunities and ran his businesses purposefully and well. He was not modest about that.
Victorians were seldom modest; they had little need
to be. So we find our subject regretting the comparative
failures of his contemporaries on the local scene with
the somewhat pedantic air of one who has harvested
the fruits of his own endeavours and concedes nothing
to the wheels of fortune.

Thus Henry Michell asserts the value of book-keeping and prides himself upon his understanding of this. He notes—and approves—Dr. Johnson's description of book-keeping as a business art. His acquisition of the Fountain Brewery in 1852 led him to attribute the failure of the Gates's business to their incompetence and having 'no business habits about them'. That, as a man of business himself was not only distressing, but inevitably disastrous. Henry Michell would never have fanned the fading embers of a dying enterprise, and he stood ready to exploit the potential asset that was his for the asking. That and his speculative initiative over the County Gaol provide good examples of Henry Michell's inexorable pursuit of business opportunities and his ability to deploy his resources and energies to advantage. There is no doubt that he felt rather superior about all this. He had reason to, for by then he had established his credentials as a successful businessman on the Horsham scene. It is surprising that he never seems to have ventured into wider fields, but his enterprise was tempered with caution as we shall see in his attitude to the railways. Aside from his book-keeping, which was no doubt adequate, I think we may reasonably attribute his success more to his native intelligence and singleness of purpose. From the start he was determined to build his business fortunes and to bequeath to his posterity an inheritance that would offer security and a desirable share of the creature comforts of life. On the face of it his interests were diversified to a considerable degree, extending to the manufacture of bricks, farming, the coal trade, and the public utilities. In fact, the foundation of his commercial strengh lay in the brewing business and its associated enterprises. He started, straight from school, in his father's business in Steyning, and soon took a post in banking as well, where his predilection for accounting doubtless served him, and his employers, well. But his ambition, and then the responsibilities he assumed on marriage could not be satisfied on such a modest managerial diet for long. He

does not say, but I imagine he was set up in the Allen
brewery by his father, a caring parental hand that he
was later to extend to his own son. At first he found it
hard going and at the end of his first full year he was
'sadly out of heart' and pocket. But he had the background and determination to establish himself within
a few years. The next year he was in the black, and in
1837 was able to place £400 to what he called Capital
Stock. This was a business surplus after all current
debts, expenses and profits had been charged. As such
it provides a convenient and reliable index of the
growth of the Michell businesses. Between 1839 and
1849 the Capital Stock account was benefiting to the
extent of about £1,000 a year. By 1857 this had risen
to £2,000, and in 1859 £2,500 was transferred to this
fund. In 1860 he was able, with the proceeds of the
gaol speculation included, to record that the accumu-
lated value of this fund had reached £30,000. He was then,
by 19th-century standards, a man of substance, and in
Horsham, rich. When, in 1862, he transferred £4,000
to Capital Stock he wondered whether it could last,
but was bound to admit that 'This seemed something like
business'. On the strength of this position he was able
to enlarge his commercial interests, and within a few
years the annual surplus had reached £5,000—'upon the
whole very satisfactory' indeed and a tribute to the
business skills upon which he justly prided himself. One
is bound to observe at this point that the preoccupation
of Henry Michell in his diary with the arithmetic of
his businesses appears to do him less than justice. Although
I have noted elsewhere that he exhibited little interest
in private or public philanthropy his evident kindness
to his family and generally liberal views do suggest that
it would be erroneous to allow this part of the diary
to dominate the personal image of Henry Michell, whose
manifest enthusiasm for his business was, nevertheless,
a cardinal feature of his personality. I have developed
this point elsewhere, but it needs reiteration before

embarking on a brief summary of the various businesses in which he was engaged.

Brewing, as I have said, was the primary source of Henry Michell's fortunes. It is also one of the ancient crafts and basic to rural life. His family were already in that business at Steyning. It was, therefore, after a brief experience in the family business and a local bank, natural that the young Henry Michell should chose that trade when the time came for him to stand on his own feet. It was thus he went to Horsham where, lacking experience as he readily acknowledges, he got off to a slow start. However, he had the drive and the confidence that comes from ability and a secure family background. He realised that the success of any manufacturer depends upon the reliability and capacity of his sales outlets which, once they will absorb the production necessary to cover the business overheads, leave the management with the surplus from which it can invest in growth and make the profits without which the enterprise cannot survive. The acquisition of *The Plough* at Three Bridges from 'one Wicks', was Henry Michell's first positive step in assuring the ultimate success of the brewing enterprise. It was a modest but intelligent venture in which he presumably foresaw the significance of the new railway which 'was set out very near it directly afterwards'. It was but the first of many others which sustained the growing output from the West Street Brewery. A beer house at West Green, near Crawley, and the *Jolly Tanner* at Staplefield Common came next. Later, among many others, he acquired *The Lamb* and *The Castle* at Horsham, the *King's Head* and *The Rising Sun* at Billingshurst, *The Wheatsheaf* at Kingsfold, *The Star* at Rusper, *The Chequers* at Rowhook, and *The King's Head* at Slinfold. Nor do I think that those public houses listed in his diary are exclusive for the Abergavenny[15] Court Books for West Chiltington show that *The Queen's Head* there was also at one time embraced in the Michell brewing empire. The same archives reveal, in a reference to a

local copyhold, that Henry Michell was Chairman of a
Horsham building society[16] in 1864, a fact that is not
mentioned in his diary from which we must conclude
there may very well be other secondary business interests
that he omitted to record.

The focus of his energies and interests was, however, the
brewery itself, and we learn from the diary how he consolidated his own position and, as opportunity offered,
redeveloped and enlarged the premises and plant. He
was methodical and prudent. Re-investment ensured
that plant was maintained and modernised and the malt
houses renewed and extended as necessary. The administration was sound and Henry Michell's own hand is
evident throughout. The capacity of one man to control
so many interests to the extent that he did reflects, not
only his own talents for business, but the relative freedom
with which the Victorian entrepreneur could operate
compared with the complexities that confront the
managers of quite small-scale businesses today. Henry
Michell's brewing business, which he conducted person-
ally for over 35 years, went from strength to strength.
Setbacks were temporary and the underlying stability
of the business ensured its steady growth. A considerable
boost resulted from the break-up of the Fountain Brewery
and the opportunities that offered for expansion. The
peak year was 1868 when Henry Michell brewed 3,075
quarters of malt; in his first year at West Street the brew
was less than 1,000 quarters; not until 1856 had the
brew reached two thousand. Many years after Henry
Michell's death Hilaire Belloc paid his unsolicited tribute
to the quality of the Michell beer in a reference to *The
Frankland Arms* at Washington in his amusing farrago
The Four Men. Later, he wrote 'the swipes[17] they take
in at the *Washington Inn* is the very best beer I know'.
The Michell company was eventually taken over by the
Rock Brewery of Brighton in 1911.

The family was in coal too, but Henry Michell's venture
into this trade was not altogether satisfactory for him.

He had had some experience of it at Steyning in his father's business and, at first he did very well in the trade that he considered he 'thoroughly understood'. The coal business thus made its due, if modest, contribution, to his commercial success. However, with the growth of the brewery interest and his increasing preoccupation with farming he decided, in 1853, that the effort involved was not justified by the financial returns. It had become a burden and he gladly laid it down.

Not so with farming, which seems to exert a universal magnetism over every career-minded man. Who has not indulged in farming fantasies at some time or another? Henry Michell was no exception. The obvious relish with which he entered this desirable state contrasts with the dour purposefulness with which he approached his other enterprises. The purchase of Staker's Farm at Southwater in 1850 was 'memorable' and clearly served as an agreeable diversion as much as anything else. Naturally, being farming there was little money in it! This did not deter him from buying Shiprods Farm at Itchingfield from John Golds 10 years later for £4,365, making what he described as 'a very important year' that 'seemed to close an old and begin a new epoch'. Farming, as it has been with others, had special satisfactions and served to mark his status in the business community. The prestige of land-owning and the preoccupation with the weather and the harvests served to gratify the parallel needs of social position, physical and mental health. It is intrinsic to the nature of farming life that it endows these rewards in a way that the less favourable image and experience of commercial business never can. Henry Michell enjoyed his farms and he soon added Dan Farm to his 'little estate'. It was a sensible and agreeable diversification of his assets.

The episode over the County Gaol was an altogether different matter. He was not in that for fun; but for money; and why not? It was there for the asking for anyone with the courage and wit to take it on. He was rather pleased too with this 'celebrated' affair and his handling of the transaction. To some extent his fortunes turned on this speculation.

The County Gaol is an interesting facet of Horsham's history. It had attracted the approving attention of none less than the penal reformer John Howard who visited the town in 1782. When, in 1845, the then redundant building was offered for sale it was Henry Michell's tender that won the day. For £2,560 he acquired an asset which he exploited with his customary energy and resource. The sale of the materials from the demolition alone netted over £5,000. The immense quantities of bricks and fittings found their way into a number of public projects in the area, including the new police station and the railway works between Horsham and Three Bridges. The debt he incurred on borrowing the money to finance this venture was cleared in two years and he went on to make a small fortune out of the property. The removal of the Assizes from Horsham in 1830 had been a matter of considerable public controversy. The demolition of the goal itself was a public spectacle and 'town talk' for many a long day. The sordid interest exhibited by Horsham people, and thousands of visitors to the town, in the former cells of the condemned prisoners' and felons' graves was perhaps inevitable. Henry Michell's generous allocation of space to this subject in his diary shows that he, too, regarded it as a landmark in his business career.

His enthusiasm for farming and speculative adventures like the County Gaol did not extend to the railways as such, although his own business interests benefited from that remarkable development. Indeed, in the case of the gaol he conceded that the demands of the railway for bricks and rubble 'came to my aid'. At one time, in 1858-9, he had to defend himself at length in the correspondence columns of the local press, against the insinuation that his support for the East Street site for the railway station was motivated by pecuniary self-interest.

The Michell inns, too, exacted their tribute from the labour that was engaged on the major construction operations in the area. Brickmaking also, in which Henry Michell was fairly heavily committed for over 20 years— he sent half a million bricks to the Crystal Palace—was stimulated by the railways which consumed large quantities for tunnelling, embankments and buildings. Yet he was sceptical about what was one of the greatest capitalist enterprises in British economic history.

In mid-Sussex the railway system as it still exists was largely laid down between 1840 and 1867. The line to Horsham from Three Bridges was completed in 1848; the link via Dorking and Warnham in 1867. The connections with the coast from Horsham were opened in 1861 to Shoreham and in 1863-4 to Littlehampton and Bognor Regis. By then the 'Railway Mania', under the economic impact of various failures as the developers over-reached themselves, had subsided. For Henry Michell it had never begun. In 1846 he records with apparent indignation a small loss on the Horsham-Guildford railway project which ran into trouble in the same year. He had only accepted a provisional directorship of this 'mad scheme' on the understanding that he would not be called upon to finance any losses, and warns the reader to avoid 'such rotten concerns'. However, he had given evidence to a parliamentary committee in support of the Bill for the main line from Three Bridges and admitted the immediate benefits to the commercial life of Horsham when it was opened in February 1848. The truth was, I think, that Henry Michell, who was keenly interested in technical progress and economic expansion, although never bitten by the railway 'bug' was strong enough when it made good business sense. What he deplored was the misguided speculation on specious prospectuses. In business he was always a model of prudence and good judgement.

The other great Victorian organisational achievement in the national economy was the development of the Public Utilities and here, too, we find Henry Michell

involved in Horsham. The town's first experience of
gas-lit[18] streets was in 1836 and Henry Michell was the
chairman of the company for over 25 years from eighteen
hundred and forty-six. He had previously been a director
and, as described in his diary, was among those who
foresaw that the fortunes of the company would depend
on enlaring its clientele through the attraction of cheaper
prices. Encouraged by the success of the Gas Company,
Henry Michell was sufficiently confident in the Waterworks[19] to invest £1,500 in 1865 and another £1,000 in
eighteen hundred and sixty-six. In recording this he writes
strongly of the public value of the undertaking and notes
the resistance, born of ignorance and prejudice, to the
supply of piped water in the town as there had been when
gas lighting was first introduced. Such is public opinion
and this comment underlies very well the merit of such
initiatives in spheres where, as Henry Michell obviously
understood, the advantages were of more lasting significance than the mere provision of an amenity.

And so we find Henry Michell's finger in many pies;
and he generally pulled out the plums as will be clear
from the business section of his diary which now follows:

> I now propose to begin a narration of my business career
> which upon the whole I must consider very satisfactory,
> although on taking a retrospective view, I can see in many
> ways how much better I could have done many things, but
> then, on the other hand, I can see a great many dangers from
> which I have been most mercifully preserved, but when I look
> back to the days of early manhood and think of those who
> started into life at the same time as myself and see what they
> have most of them done, I may well be thankful. I should
> be sorry to draw too gloomy a picture of the progress of
> my compeers in early life, but I fear I do not exaggerate at
> all when I say that not one in ten have prospered in the sense
> in which that term is generally used. Now there must be
> some reason for this, and I believe it is to be found in defective
> training of young lads in their business, moral, and physical
> pursuits. As regards business, the science of bookkeeping
> is above and beyond everything necessary to success. I was
> always impressed with the importance of this branch of

education, and I well remember when my master (Mr. Gandell of Pulboro) urged my Father to send me back to him again for one more half year for the purpose of learning it, and he refused, I was sorely tried, but men who do not understand bookkeeping don't know the value of it, and my Father thought I must know all about it because I was a tolerable Arithmetician.

I hardly know when my business life began, as on leaving school I assisted my Father in the general management of the Brewery, Malting and Coal businesses at Steyning, and I had something to do with Farming as well. This continued for several years up to Jany. 1833, when I accepted the management of Messrs. Henty and Upperton's Bank at Steyning which they honored me with the offer of. I was now in that position for which I seemed to have been born, so thoroughly in accordance with my very nature and instincts was the general character and details of the banking business. I went into the Office to supersede a Mr. Moore on the 1st. of January, and in about 2 months I could manage the whole system of bookkeeping very easily, and I rarely had any error in my balance, but I now sometimes think I was wanting in deference and was very conceited and independent to my employers, but still I am bound in justice to myself to say that they never expressed any dissatisfaction with me. My office hours were by no means a great confinement and only 3 days per week, so that I could assist my Father in his business as well. The Salary I received was £80 a year with which I was perfectly satisfied .

I was sensible enough to see I was gaining valuable experience in business generally, as well as in bookkeeping, which Dr. Johnson says 'is an art which must contribute to the advancement of all who buy and sell; of all who wish to keep or improve their possessions; of all who desire to be rich, and all who desire to be wise'. From my own experience in business, and also what I have seen and heard of as the cause of commercial panics, bankrupt merchants, and crashing Banks, I can fully endorse every word of the learned Dr. on this subject.

I continued in my situation at Steyning till August 1834, when I left to get married and begin business in this town of Horsham and on these very premises now called Grandford House and including the Literary Institution as well, where the brewing business had for many years been carried on by Mr. W. Allen, who let it to me on Lease for 7 years. I, or I should rather say we (I always looked to my dear Wife for help in trouble) were now fairly embarked in the battle of life and well do I remember the hopes and fears, the doubts and difficulties with which our progress in business was beset. Sometimes the competition seemed overwhelming and then the very elements seemed combined against us in bad or difficult harvests, but I can now see that all this was no more than all my rivals had to contend with as well as myself, and that the only way to overcome them is to rise betimes in the morning and combat and settle every difficulty, lay every ghost, as it makes it appearance, let every day bear its own burden. I think I shall best carry out my intentions in these memoirs by relating the chief events affecting our business career as they occurred year by year. We began brewing on these premises in Jany. 1835. The mash vat[20] stood in the middle of what is now the assembly room of the literary institution; the horse wheel was in the library and passage, the copper was in an arch over the stairs, and the coolers where the ante-room is now; the cleansing rooms under this and a long building running up the garden and joining a large building erected by Mr. Thornton about 1780 as a school-room. Of course a great deal of all this is pulled down and some part very much altered to adapt it to its present purpose. Of all the facts connected with business, I never remember one more fully impressed on my mind than that first day's brewing, as I had not had sufficient practical experience to feel confidence in myself, and I have no doubt now it would have answered well to have engaged a thorough practical Brewer to manage this part of the business. I did sometimes very well, then another time very unsatisfactorily without knowing the cause of the failure, but one thing I well remember and that was the delight with which I carried home (we were lodging for a short time at Mr. George Sheppards near the Town Hall) the first money, about 40s. received for grains and a few eggs the hens had laid, and very soon this was followed by a little yeast money as well. It seemed as if some at least of the money we had laid out in getting here was coming back. I was using at this time a Malthouse at Gay street,[21] near Adversane, but this was very much out of the way and so I gave it up as soon as I could, and took an old house in Billingshurst Street, now pulled down. I found the trade for Beer not very brisk and brewed the first year only about 400 quarters. No doubt if I had understood the business better I could have done much more, but I also entered into the coal trade, and this I may say, I thoroughly understood. I took the wharf at Bines bridge entirely into my own hands, and very soon did a large trade, comparatively, at any rate. I did more than all the other merchants put together.

One day in the month of April this year I took a ride to Crawley and the neighbourhood and called at an old publick house at the Three Bridges (corner of Hazelwick mill lane) called the Plough, kept by one Wicks, who told me the house with 12 acres of land belonged to his family and was for sale. I subsequently bought it for £700, which proved very cheap, as the Railway was set out very near it directly afterwards. It was, indeed, a most fortunate purchase. I began brick-making on the ground in 1838 and made a great many for the railway in 1839, which, however, turned out an unfortunate speculation, but I afterwards let it at a remunerative rent and very soon was applied to to sell some of the land for building.

I now resumed the brickmaking again myself, and ultimately made £1000 by it. I also have sold off land amounting to about £   . The rent has always more than amounted to a fair per centage on the first purchase, in addition to a good trade for Beer. I think I am quite within the mark if I say this little property, the first I purchased, resulted in a clear profit to us from first to last amounting to nearly or quite £5000. I also bought about this time a beer house at West Green, near Crawley. I gave £200 for it and laid out some money on it. It proved a very advantageous purchase and with the old Plough gave me quite a footing in that neighbourhood and laid the foundation of much more business.

There was a very good crop of barley this year and the harvest was excellent. The average price of barley was 35s. per quart. Hops, too, were plenty and cheap and the profits on brewing were consequently very good where any amount of business could be done. I was sadly out of heart on making up my books to the 31st. of December to see I was £176 over the left, or wrong side.

1836. This year was marked by nothing particular in the business. We Brewed a little over 600 quarters of Malt at 60s. per quarter. Hops were about £6 per cwt. The profits were consequently pretty good per quarter brewed, and we also did more in the coal trade, and the winding up showed a balance of £311 on the right side.

Balance in favour of Beer account £1312.

1837. Brewed this year 750 Qr. of Malt at 60s. per quarter Hops were about 1d. per lb. Balance in favour of Beer £1560, and the balance on the profit and Loss account as carried clear profit to Capital stock £400.

This year I bought the Jolly Tanner at Staplefield Common for £400. I was offered £50 more for it before I left the sale room. This proved a great bargain, as it has always yielded £5 per cent interest, besides a good Beer trade. I began brick making.

1838. Brewed this year 766 quarters at 60s. per quarter. Hops cost 1d. per lb. Balance on the Beer account £1733; clear profit carried to capital stock £500. Bought the Adversane public house of Mr. R. Watkins for £750, a very harmless bargain, but useful as an addition to our trade.

Began Brick making (Kiln Bricks) at the Three Bridges this year. There was every prospect of a ready for sale for them, as the Brighton railway was about to be begun. The first brick of the observatory on the summit of Balcombe tunnel was laid on the same day.

Queen Victoria was crowned June 28, 1838.

1839. Brewed this year 1175 quarters, the price of which was 64s. to 66s. per quarter for the make of 1838-9. In consequence of a very bad harvest barley was inferior in quality and much dearer than it had been for several seasons, and when new malt had to be had recourse to in November, it could not be obtained at less than 70s. per quarter. Hops were fortunately very cheap, about 60s. to 70s. per cwt.

The balance on the Beer account was £2669, and the clear profit carried to Capital stock £1000.

The Brighton railway was now in full operation in construction and was the cause of the sudden increase in our business. I had also a great many men at work in making bricks at the Three bridges, but this turned out a very unfortunate speculation. My foreman cheated me in every way; I had placed every confidence in him as he had been recommended to me by Mr. Kemp of Uxbridge. I, of course, knew nothing of the business myself. The very elements seemed to have conspired against brick making this summer; large quantities were washed down in the hack, and the fires were put out in the clamps before the bricks were sufficiently burned. This, of course, was a great loss as there was then a duty on bricks of 5s. 10d. per 1,000 and I paid nearly £500 duty for the summer of 1839. It was altogether most discouraging. The

Railway contractors would not buy my bricks till they were compelled to do so, or let their works stand still. I ultimately sold a good many at a very high price and so I eventually cleared out at a loss of only a few hundreds pounds, whereas at one time it threatened to be almost ruinous.

1840. Brewed this year 1404 quarters at 70s. per quarter, and very inferior in quality too, as the barley of 1839 being very much injured by wet during the harvest, there was hardly such a thing to be found as a sample of dry, bright corn of any description. I recollect hearing that in Wales nearly all the wheat was carried into the cattle yards; it was perfectly useless for human food and I know that barley was bought in Pulboro market for shipment to Wales to make bread of from causes before stated.

The balance on the beer account was only £2640 and nothing was carried to the Capital stock account, but £1140 was carried forward in favour of profit and loss account to cover or meet heavy losses anticipated on many of the Railway beer accounts and some on the brick concern, but much more to meet the heavy expense of removing the Brewery plant from Allen's premises to the West Street Brewery, which was now arranged to be carried out in the spring of the ensuing year (1841).

1841. Brewed this year 1031 quarters at an average price of 60s. per quarter. The harvest 1840 was very good and barley was good in quality and very moderate in price as shown by the price of Malt, but it is an old saying and was proved true this year that a good Hop and Barley year never come together. The hop crop of 1840 was very short, paying only £34,000 duty, consequently the extra price of hops was equal to an extra cost of at least 5s. per quarter for every quarter of Malt brewed. The balance in favour of Beer account carried to the profit and loss account was £2127. The cost of moving the Brewery plant to the West Street Brewery which was very nearly, or quite £1000, prevented anything being carried as clear profit to the Capital Stock account this year, but £557 was carried forward to the credit of profit and loss account for next year.

The cost of removal seemed to be a great sacrifice, but I had no alternative, as Mr. Allen was a man it was impossible to do business with on any fair terms, and in giving up these premises I also had to give up three public houses rented with them, viz. the Dog and Bacon Inn, Horsham, the Compasses at Alfold, and the Kings head at Billingshurst; this with the decrease of trade consequent on the completion of the London & Brighton Railway greatly diminished the business prospects for the future. However, I was so well pleased with the new premises and the terms upon which I held them from Sir Timothy Shelley, that I was in high spirits at our future prospects, and here I must relate an anecdote of my interview with Sir Timothy Shelley at Field place when I applied to him to Let me the West Street Brewery, then in possession of Mr. Rawlinson, though dismantled as a Brewery.

I think it was in the Autumn of 1840 I went to Field place. On being introduced to Sir Timothy, he said, 'And who are you?' I told him my name was Michell, that my grandfather was the late Mr. Michell of Hermonger's. He replied by saying, 'Oh you are? Why, I shot with him and partook of his hospitality 70 years ago, and a very respectable man he was too'. I was quite delighted to find I had touched a chord to which he so cheerfully responded, and he at once said he saw no reason why my application should not be acceded to.

1842.   Brewed this year 838 quarters at 64. per quarter up to the new malt when the price fell to 60s. per quarter, the balance of Beer account carried to profit and Loss account was £1713. I carried nothing this year as clear profit to Capital Stock, but the balance of profit and Loss account carried to 1843 amounted to £841.

I have nothing particular to record this year relative to the business which was considerably less than that of the year preceding, from the loss of Allen's houses and the decline in the railway trade.

The harvests of 1841 and 1842 were very good as proved by the prices charged for Malt: as stated above, it was a remarkably fine summer all through and a wonderful year for fruit. I remember we had about 45 gallons of grapes brought home from the old Malt house at Billingshurst and I trode them out in a tub and there were 27 gallons of juice which I put into a 36 Gn. cask and filled it up with sugar and a little water. This wine was like syrup at 20 years old. The crop of Apples was very great and fine.

The average price of barley for the season 1842-3 was 31s. per qr.

1843. Brewed this year 731 quarters of Malt at 60s. per Quarter, the balance of Beer account carried to Profit and Loss was £1926, the profit on coals and malting amounted together to £623; this with the balance brot forward from 1842 enabled me to carry £1000 to the Capital Stock account on the 31st. of December. The harvest of this year was very good, and the price of corn very moderate. The average of barley was for season 1843-4 32s. 4d. per quarter. The books do not show any transaction during the year to require comment. The balance on the profit and loss account carried forward to 1844 was £554.

1844. Brewed this year 834 quarters at 60s. per quarter, except the last 100 quarters of new malt at 64s. The balance carried to P. & L. account was £1905; although nearly 100 quarters more malt was brewed than last year, the profit was less owing to the high price of hops. The profit on coals and Malting was £518. I carried £500 to the capital stock account and the balance carried forward was only £141 to the credit of Profit and loss account for 1845. I charged £445 to P. and L account this year as money sunk on a house I built at the north end of Balcombe tunnel called the Rastrick Arms for the Railway trade and several other considerable losses on book debts.

1845. Brewed this year 830 quarters at 64s. per quarter. The balance carried to Profit and Loss from the beer account was £1782. The profit on coals and malting together was £597. Carried to Capital Stock account £437. 17. 6, which made a total of profit from the brewing, Malting and Coal business (from the commencement) of £4000, and this after covering the loss sustained the first year.

This year is celebrated in my business career for having become the purchaser by tender of the County Gaol which stood in what was formerly known as the Causeway croft in East Street. My tender was for £2560. The tenders were opened before a full meeting of all the magistrates of the county at Lewes in October 1845. I was present and was delighted to hear my name mentioned by the Earl of Chichester, the chairman, as the purchaser. I had every reason to believe it was a great bargain as the amount of materials was, I may say, vast; but the expense of realizing was great and arduous. After disposing of the material, I bought some other land adjoining and added to the site

They paid me £1000 for what they took, and left the rest on my hands to dispose of as I could. Some I sold for building, on a part of it I built the new Malt house, and some I sold to the Waterworks Company and some I hold still. I suppose from the first to last I made about ten millions of bricks on the ground and I consider it has resulted altogether, with the ground still on hand, in a profit to me of at least £5000. I never look back on this transaction with any other feelings than of pride and satisfaction, and often wonder how I could have had courage enough to enter into it, and particularly as I had no capital to spare, and I borrowed every shilling of the purchase money of my Bankers by promissory note at 3 months, paying off as much as I could every time it was renewed, and so I cleared it all off in about 2 years, and then of course I could see that what was left of the material with the ground was clear profit, whatever that might turn out to be worth, which ended better than my most sanguine estimate had led me to expect. I should here state that the site of the Gaol together with the meadow at the back and some ground on which was carried on the business of a stone mason and Builder on the West side (both of which I purchased of Mr. Padwick) was all thrown together and called Park square, but as the Railway went right through it and left some on one side and some on the other, it was afterwards called Park square East, and Park square west. Thinking the character of the structure of the Gaol might some future day be matter for speculation among natives yet unborn, I had several sketches taken of it by Mr. Thos. Honeywood, and I have even now great reason to be glad I did so, as I often find them useful to refer to. The sketch of the governor's house with a part of the boundary wall is perhaps the most interesting as showing the elevation of the general structure from the road. On the back of this is a very complete ground plan of the whole pile. It was built in 1775 and one man, a Mr. Sharp, called in one day and said he witnessed the building of it, and then certainly never thought he should live to see it pulled down.

I obtained possession of the Gaol the beginning of November and the St, Leonards Fair[22] was held near the Queen's head on the 17th. of November and as I allowed any one to go over it (in fact I threw it quite open to public view) and thousands of people flocked to see it, (there were very few, even in the town of Horsham who had ever gone over it) and I was called upon to give my personal attendance to so many of my own friends and also to reiterate an explanation of the different parts of the building and the purpose to which each was applied from the 'condemned cell' to the murderers' grave, that I got quite tired of it and was enabled to form some idea of the life of a showman.

1846.   Brewed this year 1022 quarters of Malt at 60s. per quarter up to the new Malt when the price rose to 68s. per quarter. The balance carried forward to profit and loss account was £2374 and from the Malting and coal business £327. £500 was added as profit this year to the capital Stock account.

I see one entry to the debit of the profit and loss account this year which merits a passing observation, and it is that of £63 on account of the Horsham & Rudgwick railway. During the Railway mania of 1845, among other mad schemes this was one, and I was asked to be a provisional director. I consented on the understanding that I was not to be liable to pay anything in any way, as I had no spare cash to invest in Railways. I was assured it would involve me in no pecuniary responsibility whatever. However, the whole thing proved a bubble which burst with the panic of 1846, and the directors, or most of them, subscribed 60 guineas each as the shortest way out of the mess. I mention this as a warning to all who may happen to read this to keep out of such rotten concerns.

The harvest this year was unusually forward, a great deal of wheat was cut and housed before our fair on the 18th. of July. I never remember such a summer for sunshine and heat. It completely scorched up the oat crop in Ireland, and occasioned which has since been known as the Irish famine, as the potatoe crop also nearly perished from some cause. The barley crop in England was materially damaged, and the market opened in October at about 45s. per quarter, and continued to advance; the last lot I bought was of W. Turner of Fittleworth at 62s. per quarter. I had none in stock, only about enough for the current year (1847), but I had no faith in the necessity of such extreme prices, and by the time I wanted to buy Malt in the Summer it was to be had at 68s. per quarter, that is, a little over what the barley cost in the Malting season—one more proof if any more were wanting, of the folly of buying any commodity when the market is excited, at least, more than is absolutely necessary.

As stated in last year I was now very busy realizing the materials of the Gaol and among other matters involved in this was the building the 'Lock up', which I agreed to do on being allowed to use all materials from the Gaol that would at all answer the purpose for about £700, about half of which was paid by the Magistrates and the remainder by the Town of Horsham and jurors attending the Sessions. The Magistrates stated they could not do with any other building than the one recommended by their surveyor, nor could they allow any more money towards it, and if the people of Horsham and the neighbourhood could not find the remainder, the midsummer sessions would be taken away from the Town, and this roused the people to action, as they did not like the idea of losing that which added a little to their importance as they thought.

It may some day be a matter of interest to some one to know a little of the materials of such a building as a county gaol and quantities contained therein. I hardly need say that Iron, stone, and Bricks and timber were the most prominent, but very little of the latter in comparison, as all the floors in the main buildings were on brick arches and paved throughout with Horsham paving stone. About 2½ million bricks were used in the building altogether and 15,000 square feet of paving stone (all Horsham stone). There were about 100 iron doors, 150 iron windows. The greater part of the old iron I sold to Palmer and Green of Brighton and I believe the Bridge which carries the Railway over the Ouse at Lewes was constructed from it. There was also a great quantity of wrought iron of the best quality which was dispersed far and wide, such was also the case with the bricks. Nearly the whole of the Railway works from the Three bridges to Horsham were constructed with them, also Moadland house and Breaches parchment factory at Steyning, and Mr. Franklyn's new house at North-lands, Warnham, and many other buildings of lesser note. I thought to give notoriety and publicity as to what materials there were for disposal I had better have an auction sale which was held by Mr. Plumer on the 24th. of February 1846, and I give as follows a few extracts from the catalogue which numbered over 500 lots.

150 8 inch iron rimd. locks
 48 Mordons patent 12 inch locks
 48 wrought iron venetian blinds
230 iron casements, sashes, and doors (of wood a few).
  7 lead pumps and 140 feet of suction pipe
  3 --- 40 step (solid stone) winding geometrical stairs.
100 (or about) sawed edge solid stone steps
1000 lineal feet of stone causeway 14 to 18 inches wide.
 80 Portland stone door jambs 5F 10in x 2.4 x 7in.
 17 iron skeleton doors.

There were several small roofs, quantities of wrought iron bricks and many other things. The whole of Park square (east and west) I sold off from the original property.

As may be supposed in demolishing a building like this there was an immense quantity of brick and mortar rubble, but in this the constructors of our railway again came to my aid, and I balasted about a mile of the railway with it. This was the year when the railway mania culminated in a regular panic. The only effect it had on my affairs was I had to pay something for my share of the liabilities incurred by the Directors of the Horsham & Guildford Railway and this was a very fortunate thing for me in one sense, as it just opened my eyes to the risks one may incur by meddling in public companies and other bubble speculations which are set on foot by a set of people who have nothing to lose themselves and are often the only gainers, if ever the concern turn out prosperously. I would therefore recommend every one not to join any company without being well satisfied that it is a sound legitimate undertaking. The Railway from the Three Bridges to this town was now the great topic of the day with commercial men here. I myself was looking forward to it with the greatest enthusiasm. The bill for it had been obtained from parliament last year (1845) and here I may remark that I and Mr. Philip Chasemore were summoned in May 1845 to give evidence before a committee in support of the bill, and most gladly did I do so and with a clear conscience.

I was now taking a very active part in the management of our gas company; having given a little more attention to the details of the process than any other director I was soon brought to the front. We were not in a very flourishing condition. I recommended the reduction of the price from 12/6d. to 8s. per 1000 cubic feet as a beginning. We soon found this was the grand secret of success as it promoted consumption to an almost unlimited extent. We have gone on reducing the price till it is now (1871) only 4s. 2d. per 1000 feet and have paid £10 per cent for years. I have been chairman of the company from the above date 1846.

1847. Brewed this year 1132 quarters of Malt, the price as may be supposed from the very high price of barley of the harvest of '46 as before stated was 80s. per quarter up to the time of obtaining Malt made from the barley of the harvest of this year, when it fell to 60s. per quarter. The balance of Beer account carried to Profit & Loss was £2700, the balance of Coals and Malting was only £246; £500 only was carried to credit of Capital Stock account, but over £300 was carried forward to credit of next year.

This was one of the most delightful years I ever remember. It was a most genial spring and the Summer was neither too wet or too dry. The weather was delightfully fine with a nice genial rain about once a week. The crop of hay was abundant and most well got; the corn crops were excellent and there was abundance of barley in Pulboro Market by the 7th. of September. I bought as much as I wanted at from 34 to 37s. per quarter. What a contrast to the state of the market the day on which I bought my last barley in the Spring preceding of Mr. Turner as narrated in 1846.

The railway from Three bridges to Horsham was begun last year, and this, was in full operation which caused a considerable accession to my business and as the harvest of this year was so good for corn and hops as well, everything looked promising for the future.

1848.   Brewed this year 1179 quarters at £3 per quarter and the profit carried to P. and L. account was £3081. The profit from the Malting and coal businesses was £420 and £1000 was carried to the Capital Stock account on the 31st of December.

The Horsham and Three bridges railway was opened in February this year; the trade of the Town felt an immediate impulse. Our trade instead of declining, as I supposed it would when the railway works were finished, continued to increase and we were now doing more than my wildest flights of imagination led me to expect and began to speculate on some day being a rich man (i.e. comparatively) if my health and strength were continued to me.

The summer of this year was altogether as wet and cold as 2 or 3 previous years had been warm and dry. The seed time in the spring was very bad and late, much of the spring corn not being sown till the beginning of May. The Hay crop was pretty good as to quantity, but much of it was damaged by the wet. The wheat harvest began about the 8th. of August and an occasional field was cleared by about the 12th. when it rained and I believe it did so every day till the first of September, when it cleared up and we had very fine weather, but all the wheat, or nearly all in this country was very much damaged, and the barley so much so as to be wholly unfit for malting, so that we had to depend entirely on Foreign supplies. Fortunately the corn laws had been repealed or relaxed, so that we could get French barley and plenty of it at about 37s. per quarter at Horsham Station.

1849.   Brewed this year 1289 quarters of Malt at 60s. per Qr. The balance carried to P. & L. account was £3001, profits from Coals and Malting £363, and the addition made to Capital Stock as profit was £1000.

We seemed now to have settled down to a pretty regular profit of £1000 a year. The barley crop was abundant this year, though not of first rate quality. The price ruled in the season 1849-50 at from 28 to 29s. a quarter, but the hop crop was very deficient; the duty was only £79,000, which was about one third of what it had been many years before. The average of the three preceding years was about 225,000 a year, so that the stock of old hops was so great that they maintained only a very moderate price.

1850.   Brewed this year 1210 quarters Malt at 56s. pr. quarter. The balance of profit carried from Beer account to Profit and Loss was £3052, from Coals and Malting £404 and the sum carried to Capital Stock was again £1000. The sum debited to P. & L. for losses on loans etc. was very heavy, being £400 this year.

I have before alluded to having bought a field at the back of the Gaol, and also a builder's yard with a cottage and orchard on the west, or two side and added the same to the ground on which the Gaol had stood (about 2 acres) and on this meadow I began brick making this summer, supposing I should sell some of the land for building and then it would be a great mutual advantage, as I should get a good profit on the bricks and the builder would be advantaged by having them close at hand. But to my surprise, I had no sooner made a quantity than parties came by rail and cleared them off as fast as we could make them, and this continued for several successive years. In 1852 we sent quite half a million to the Crystal palace at Sydenham. I also began brick making again about this time at the Three bridges, and continued it for several years. I sustained a considerable loss by some speculative builders at Reigate in 1854 and 5, but with this exception I was very fortunate and in the end cleared nearly £3000. I also began about this time to sell more of the land at the Three bridges for building and of course the purchasers were glad to buy bricks on the spot. This year I bought the Leases of the Lowfield heath and Leigh houses.

The harvest this year was very good indeed, but barley was light, the general weight being about 50 lbs. per bushel, but the price was low enough. I bought 1058 quarters at 26s. 5d. per quarter average price. The crop of hops was very large, duty £233,393.

This year is also memorable in my business annals for having taken Stakers farm, which was quite a new thing for me and more conducive to my health than money profit.

1851.   Brewed this year 1300 quarters of Malt at 54s. per quarter, excepting 250 quarters of new which was charged at 50s. The profit carried to Profit and Loss account was £3058 and that from Coals and Malting was £408. The sum added to Capital Stock was £1000.

The summer of 1851 was a remarkable fine time; the crops of every description were good, excepting hops, which was middling. The duty was £130,053; the barley crop was very good and in the malting season 1851-2 I bought 1258 quarters at about 30s. pr. quarter. I remember almost the last I bought was of my own Father on the 31st. of March 21½ quarters at 34s. per quarter. It was beautiful in quality and weighed about 56 lbs. per bushel. It grew on land he used in Steyning lanes and I recollect his saying he grew more than 8 quarters of it to the acre.

1852.   Brewed this year 1371 quarters of Malt at 56s. per quarter. The balance carried to profit and Loss account was £2956. The balance from coals and Malting was £463. The balance added to Capital Stock was £1000.

The harvest this year was good altogether, though I remember there was a very heavy shower or two which made some of the wheat grow in the sheaf, but the barley must have been well got, but it was light, hardly any weighing more than 51 or 52 lbs. per bushel. The price was very moderate. I bought in the season 1852-3, 1357 quarters at an average of 30s. 1d. per quarter.

The great event to us in business this year was the breaking up of the Messrs. Gates business at the Fountain Brewery. Hitherto I don't know that I have alluded to them. I always looked upon them as rivals deserving more pity than blame, having a practical knowledge of their business and no business habits about them. For some years they had been tottering to their fall and it was evident to the initiated that every step they took to improve their position only hastened their final doom. I think they suspended business in 1851; their public house property was sold this year and the brewery with these premises then known (in conjunction with what is now the Literary institution) as the Richmond Hotel, in 1853. The Fountain Brewery was carried on on the premises next to this house on the West side and is now occupied by Mr. W. Holden. Mr. George Marshall of Godalming had a lien upon the whole concern, and he made it his business to call on me and say that any amount which I would like to purchase he would let all or any part of the money lay on my giving him my bond and depositing the Deeds of the property as security. I need hardly say this suited my book exactly, and I availed myself of it to the extent of between five and six thousand pounds for which I purchased 'the Kings head Inn', Billings-hurst, the Queen's head Inn, Itchingfield, the Wheat Sheaf Inn, Kingsfold, the Lamb Inn, Horsham, and the Parrot Inn, Abinger, and also the Fountain Brewery and these premises as before stated.

Of course all these houses added to our business as well as many other customers in consequence of the stoppage of the Fountain Brewery seemed a great addition to our business, and it was evident I must make some fresh arrangement for enlarging the Brewery, and I thought a more convenient and spacious Malthouse might be connected with it. I therefore drew up a plan of such a building as I thought would answer the purpose and submitted it to Sir Percy Shelley, and he decided upon accepting my offer to construct the whole of it for £1000 and pay an additional rent of £60 per annum. It was to be done under the superintendence and to the satis-faction of Mr. John Honeywood. I think I may say this enlargement of the Brewery was carried out to the entire satisfaction of all parties. It gave us much more room in the Brewery and enabled me to carry on the Malting business under my own eye, and I of course at once gave up the old wretched Malthouse I had used for many years in Billings-hurst Street and also the house situated opposite the Barrack fields in the Worthing road.

1853.   Brewed this year 1474 quarters malt. About 1201 of
it was charged at 56s. per quarter and the remainder at 68
per quarter. The profit carried to P. & L. was £3888, that
from Coals and Malting £333 and the sum added to Capital
stock was £1000.

This was altogether one of the very wettest years I ever
remember, and consequently we had a very short crop of
corn of every description. It began raining very much in the
spring of 1852, but there were intervals of fine weather which
allowed of the hay and corn to be got in pretty well this
year as before stated, but about Michaelmas it set in so wet
as to interfere very materially with the wheat sowing. There
were a few fine days the beginning of October when I got my
wheat put in at Stakers farm. All who missed that opportunity
had no other till the spring, the consequence was the lain of
wheat was very short, and a great deal of that did not yield
8 bushels per acre. Many many small farmers I knew had no
more than enough for their family consumption and to seed
their ground again. I was more fortunate than any one
adjoining my farm at Stakers, and yet I grew only 56 sacks
of wheat on 20 acres. The Barley crop was deficient and very
much damaged by the wet. It was so backward, too. I was
shooting at Whipley on the first of September, and only
a small part of the barley crop had been got in; a great deal
was in swarth and growing very fast as it laid, and much was
not yet cut. In the following season, 1853-4, I bought 1450
quarters at an average of little under 40s., the weight was
very low—about 49 to 52 lbs. per bushel, and the quality
altogether very inferior.

The hop crop this year was middling, the duty being
£152,000. This was altogether a very busy year with me as
before stated. I bought the Fountain Brewery this year and
then I bought a great part of the plant of Gates' trustees and
Mr. Taunton, who was then using the Brewery and all this I
had to convert into cash, and I got a little more than I gave
for it, but it was a very harmless affair either one way or
the other. My next step was to convert the premises into
their present form or something very near it, in order to make
a rent of it, and I let it to Mr. Sadler, Solicitor.

I was also very much engaged in carrying out the new
arched cellars with the Malthouses over them alluded to in
the latter part of my last year's narrative. I had to make
the bricks (which I did on the ground lately occupied by the
Gaol) and build the place ready for use by the commencement of the malting season.

As I·found the Brewery business was constantly increasing and might be made to pay better by directing more attention to it, I resolved upon giving up the coal trade as it involved a great deal of labour at a very small profit, and the men engaged in it were really never fit to be sent out with beer. This step met with the hearty concurrence of my wife as well as of every one in my employ, and I can say with truth I have never once regretted it.

1854. Brewed this year 1830 quarters malt at 70s. per quarter, the profit carried to Profit and Loss account was £4098, the profit from Malting £285 and the sum added to Capital Stock was again £1000.

This year the Crimean War broke out and there was an additional duty of 10s. per quarter immediately put on Malt, and that detracted very much from the profits of the Beer, as it was impossible to charge a corresponding price or make an adequate difference in the quality, and in addition to this, I sunk as much as £500 in building and furnishing the new cellars and Malthouses. But for these causes I should have have had at least £500 more to add to capital stock, and as they were exceptional, I think it right to name it here.

The harvest this year was excellent and the crops of every description of grain were good. I bought in the malting season 1854-5, 1373 quarters of barley at 34/6d. per quarter, and it was as good in quality as it was reasonable in price, but the extra Malt duty as stated above made Malt come rather dear nevertheless. The old saying that a good barley year and a good hop year seldom come together was realized this year, as the latter came very short and paid only £47,000 duty.

1855. Brewed this year 1734 quarters of Malt, 1418 quarters were charged at 70s per quarter and 316 at 76s. The balance carried to Profit and Loss was £3791 and from Malting £420, and £1,000 was again added to Capital Stock account.

There is nothing particular to record of this years business, excepting we were very busy in the brick line.

This could not be called a very prolific year. I believe the wheat crop was very good and all corn was pretty well harvested, but the barley was very inferior; it was short in quantity and very inferior in quality, most of it weighing only from 51 to 53 lbs. per bushel, not much of the latter weight. I bought 1551 quarters at an average of 39/9 per quarter. Fortunately the Crimean War was terminated this year and the duty was relegated to its former amount, but of course the high price of Malt and the secondary quality together materially lessened the balance carried to the profit and Loss account.

The crop of hops was enormous, paying £398,635 duty, the largest by 70,000 ever recorded. This was in favour of next year's operations.

1856.   Brewed this year 2103 quarters of Malt at an average price of 74s. per quarter; the balance carried to profit and Loss account being £4662, and that from the Malting £530. The sum added to Capital Stock was again £1000, which would have been more, but taking advantage of a larger amount of business having been done, I took the opportunity to charge the profit and loss account with £500 as depreciation of Leaseholds and several small securities of very doubtful validity or ultimate value.

The harvest was very bad this year: we had a very fine summer and the crops were luxuriant and promising, but just as a good deal of wheat was cut and the barley too, it began to rain in violent thunder storms so that the corn very quickly sprouted.

I bought in the Malting season 1856-7, 2243 quarters of barley at an average of very nearly 45s, per quarter; it was so sprouted that it weighed only from 50 to 52 lbs. per bushel, and made the most wretched malt I ever brewed. One of the worst features in the character of the barley was the effect of the heavy showers and hot sun, which caused it all but to germinate, but not quite, so that it could not be detected in the sample, but it grew very badly on the Malthouse floors and some of the beer was more like barley water than Ale or beer. The crop of hops this year was again very good, the duty being £266,899.

1857. Brewed this year 2445 quarters of malt at 72s. per quarter. The balance carried to profit and loss account was £5097 and from the Malting £424, and £2000 was now added to the Capital Stock fund.

This year I bought the Castle Inn, West Street, for £700 and the Star, Horsham Common for £430.

The harvest this year was much better than 1856, but there were many sprouted samples of grain this year, but the barley was much better and weighed generally from

52 to 54' lbs. per bushel. I bought 2720 quarters of barley in the season 1857-8 at an average of about 39/6d. per quarter; upon the whole the crops were good.

The crop of hops this year was very large, the duty amounting to £228,294.

1858.   Brewed this year 2243 quarters of Malt at an average of 62s. per quarter. The balance carried to Profit and loss account was £5326, and the profit of the Malting was £500 and sum carried to Capital Stock was £2000 after charging several heavy losses, and I sunk a good deal this year in repairs of old houses and additions to plant and rolling stock to meet the requirements of a constantly increasing business.

I bought the Star Inn, Rusper this year of Charles Read for £1,250.

I have this year to record the treaty with the Mid Sussex Railway Company for the ground they took from me in Park square, for which they paid me £1,000, and very lucky I was to get it, as many of those who gave up their land without the money had a great deal of trouble and some of them lost it through the bankruptcy of the Solicitor and contractor. This was a very prosperous year altogether. The Mid Sussex railway in full operation; there was plenty of trade—beer, bricks and building ground—and everything was going ahead and Malt and hops were cheap. The crop of the latter was again enormous, the duty paying £254,000.

The corn harvest this year was very good, and well got in, but the barley was light. I bought in the season 1858-9, 2660 quarters at an average of 35s. 3d. per quarter. The general weight was 52lbs. per bushel.

1859.   Brewed this year 2369 quarters of Malt at 64s. per quarter. The balance carried to profit and loss account was £5169, and the profit on Malting was £758. I was now using the Malthouse at Rock, and had been for 3 or 4 years. The sum added to Capital Stock this year was £2500. I again sunk £300 in Leaseholds and losses in bad debts, etc and purchased the Rising Sun, Billingshurst for £260, and the Dun horse Inn and cottages for £850, but I subsequently sold a part of the latter to P. Goldsmith for £200. I also bought the meadows at Polecats, Nuthurst, of James Killick for £400 and subsequently sold a part of the same to the Railway (Horsham and Shoreham line) for £155, a part to

Gibbs of Farley house for £325, and the remainder to Sir P. Burrell for £100, thereby clearing £180 by this little property in about a year.

Our business seemed now settled down to require more Malt, a good deal than could be made at the Brewery Malthouse and as the house at Rock was very ill arranged and inconvenient, either to get barley to it, or Malt from it, I came to the conclusion it would be better at once to build such a house as should set this question at rest for some time to come. I therefore studied the matter of construction, and the result was the building the new Malthouse in Park square close to the railway, capable of making nearly 2000 quarters a year. I drew the whole of the plans and made the estimates myself. The cost, allowing £100 for site, was £1500.

The weather this summer was intensely hot. The hay crop was very short; the corn crops generally were pretty good, but barley was inferior. I malted nearly all Danish which was better than usual. I malted 2185 quarters at an average of 35/6d. per quarter, and it weighed 55 lbs. per bushel. The hop crop was next to the largest ever known, duty £328,070.

1860.   Brewed this year 2285 quarters at about 65s. per quarter. The balance carried to Profit and loss account was £5502, and from the Malting £676. I also cleared up the hop account which yielded a profit of £500, and the bricks 1000, and the real estate account which yielded a balance chiefly from the sale of ground for building purposes at the 3 Bridges, and partly from the profit of the Polecat meadows, before alluded to, and some from this (then known as the Richmond house and Fountain Brewery property) and then £200 from the gaol ground and material, altogether making an addition of £7100 to the capital stock account, which now amounted independent of borrowed capital, to just £30,000 comprised as follows:—

H.M. private property	...	...	2,400
Profit & Loss account	...	...	22.900
Gaol profit	...	...	2,200
Brick do	...	...	1,000
Hop do.	...	..	500
3 Bridges & other property	...		1,000
Total	...	...	£30,000

This was a very important year in my business concerns and seemed to close an old and begin a new epoch. I bought

Shiprods farm of John Golds this year for £4365, and also built the new Malthouse alluded to in last year's affairs. I also bought the Queen's head Inn, Bucks Green, for £700. Altogether it was a very busy and prosperous year.

The weather this year was the coldest and wettest I ever remember. The harvest was very backward, reaping was not general before the first of September, and a great deal of the corn was very much injured, particularly the barley which sprouted in the field a good deal. Nearly the whole of the barley I malted in this season 1860-1 was from Denmark or Scotland, 2534 quarters at 43s. per quarter, and weighed only 52 lbs. per bushel.

The crop of hops was very small, the duty being only £53,485, but I was fortunate in holding a good stock, and I had about 100 pockets to sell. I sold 53 pockets in one deal with Mr. A. Agate at about £10 per cwt. The amount of the invoice was £714, out of which I cleared £400 clear profit.

1861. Brewed this year 2653 quarters of Malt, nearly all of it at a cost of 72s. per quarter. The balance carried to credit of Profit and loss account from the Beer account was £5751, and from the Malting £518, and the balance carried to debit of Capital Stock account was £2,500. I sunk considerable money this year year in remodelling and enlarging the Brewery and adapting the plant to boiling and heating the liquor by steam, and I believe I succeeded in constructing a Brewery all but perfection, as there was no pumping anywhere from the time the hot liquor was first let on the goods to the racking the beer in the cellar.

This was a tolerably fine summer; the crops of corn were pretty good, though the quality of the barley was not first rate, but pretty well harvested. I bought in the season 1861-2, 3016 quarters at 36s. 6d. per quarter, and the weight was 51 to 53 lbs. per bushel. The crop of hops this year was about half a good fair crop, duty paid £114,000, and this year is memorable as being the last in which any duty was charged on hops.

I had no matter of finance of any great importance this year, excepting the purchase of the St. Leonards Hotel, which I bought of Alfred Rewell for £1000.

I began making bricks and drain pipes at Shiprods this year very early, and did a good deal in draining the land and renewing the buildings, both of which wanted doing bad enough. I am quite satisfied from my experience of this

Farm that such land will not bear any rent at all if it is not
drained. As an example, the Church meadow this year bore
only 4 loads of very inferior grass, and for many subsequent
years 8 loads was the least we ever carried off it; several times
it yielded 10 or 12 loads, and once, in 1869, 18 loads.

1862.   Brewed this year 2777 quarters of Malt at 65s. per
quarter. The balance carried to Profit and Loss account was
£6547 and from the Malting £764, and the profit added to
Capital Stock was £4000. This seemed something like business,
and I could not make up my mind that this would last, as
I concluded that brick making and railway works would
decline as a matter of course, but time has proved that, though
my anticipations were to some extent correct, I was over
sensitive on this point; but I suppose it is only natural if we
acquire a position of success beyond what we had ever
imagined that we are then in fear something will arise to
disturb the security created by it.

It was altogether a very fine summer and an excellent
harvest. I bought in the season 1862-3, 3213 quarters of
barley at an average of 35s. 6d. per quarter; the general
weight was 52½ lbs. per bushel. The crop of hops this year
was very fair, but there was no longer any duty charged by
which it could be measured.

I bought Dan farm this year of Mr. John Sayres for £1500
and the timber was valued at £600. This was a very satisfactory purchase, as it made our little estate very complete
both in an agricultural and sporting point of view, and as land
sells, it was a very reasonable price, as the buildings are so
good; in fact, when they were built by this Mr. Sayres's
father about 50 years ago, they were said to have cost more
than half what I gave for the whole farm.

1863.   Brewed this year 2797 quarters of Malt at 64s. and
52s. per quarter (500 quarters at the latter price). The
balance carried to Profit and Loss Account was £6806, and
from the Malting £791, and the profit added to Capital Stock
account was £3500. The cost of hops was 6/6d. per quarter.
This was altogether a very fine summer; the Wheat and barley
and other corn was all carted in very good condition. I bought
in the Malting season 1863-4, 2791 quarters of barley at an
average price of 35/9d. per quarter and the weight about 54
to 55 lbs. per bushel.

1864. Brewed this year 2866 quarters of Malt at 62s. per quarter and the balance carried to the Profit and Loss account was £8729, nearly £1000 more than it had ever been, which arose from the greater quantity brewed, and the reduced price of malt and also hops, the cost of which was 5/9 per quarter.

The amount of clear profit carried to the Capital Stock account was £5,000, an unusual sum, but this was a very fine summer and year altogether. Business was brisk, and everything prospered. The Malting business only paid £509 this year. The barley of the harvest of 1863 was very good, but I think I gave the beer trade all, or the greater part of the advantages by charging a very low price for the Malt. As I have said before, this was one of the finest summers I ever remember and the crops of corn were first rate, both in quantity . . .

In the Malting season 1864-5 we bought Qrs. 3351 of barley at an average of 30s. 9d. per quarter and the weight was from 54 to 56 and 57 and 58 lbs. per bushel. Taking the weight and price together, this was the best year for barley I had ever experienced. The crop of hops was also very good, at any rate, the price was moderate.

I made no investment of any amount this year. The only addition to real property being the Fox and hounds at Picts hill, which I bought for £500.

I also built the Station Hotel, Arundel this year at a cost altogether of about £1800.

1865. Brewed this year 2778 quarters of Malt at 60s. per quarter and the balance carried to the Profit and Loss account was £7798, and that from the Malting was £1000. The cost of hops per quarter of Malt was 6/2d.

The amount of clear profit carried to the Capital Stock was £4000, which I was very well satisfied with, as I incurred rather more losses than usual in the shape of bad debts and writing off one or two small loans which had lapsed, and another very important item over the left was £140 to house-keeping account as expenses for our second Foreign tour, which we made this year, and during which we had the most lovely weather imaginable. It was altogether a very fine summer and the crops of corn and everything else were good, but Malting barley was not very plentiful owing to a little rain which caught it in swarth, but the supply of both French and Scotch was very good, and we bought principally of those, altogether 2770 quarters at an average of 36s. 7d.

and the weight of Scotch was 55 lbs. but English and French
did not weigh more than from 50 to 52½ lbs. per bushel.
This year I invested £1500 in the Horsham Waterworks.
I have taken a great interest in this matter as I think it is
very much wanted and I have no doubt but in the end it will
pay very well, but the ignorance and prejudice one meets
with in offering this, one of the greatest necessities of nature
both in a physical and moral sense, from those who ought
to hale it as a great boon, is surprising and disheartening,
but there was just as much ill-feeling against Gas when that
was first established here. I also bought the King's head,
Slinfold this year for £1000 and £100 for inventory of fix-
tures etc.

The crop of hops was not so very good this year as the price
next year will testify.

1866.   Brewed 2977 quarters at 65s. per quarter and the
balance carried to profit and loss account was £8225, the
cost of hops this year was about 8s. 4d. per Qr. The profit
from Malting was £817.

The amount carried to Capital Stock account from Profit
and loss as clear profit was £5000.

We had a very nice spring and summer up to the beginning
of September. Nearly or quite all the corn was got in in
good order in the south of England, but the barley was very
inferior and weighed only from 51 to 53 lbs. per bushel. We
used most Holstein barley in the season 1866-7, bought
altogether 2705 quarters at an average price of 43s. 4d. per
quarter. This taking the quality and price into consideration
was a very high price and one of the dearest years I ever knew,
but a large breadth of the barley in the Midland counties
and a good deal in Norfolk was all but spoiled from the
incessant rains which set in the beginning of September.
The crop of Hops was very much injured from the same
cause.

I did not make any purchase of real property this year,
but invested £1000 more in the Horsham Waterworks
company; this made £2500 in all, £1000 of which I took as
ordinary shares, and the £1500 I lent on the promissory
of the Directors at £4 per cent.

1867.   Brewed this year 2823 quarters of Malt at a cost
of 70s. per quarter, the balance carried to profit and loss
account was £7124, and that from Malting was £717; the cost
of hops this year was quite 10/6 per quarter of Malt.

The amount carried to Capital Stock account from Profit and loss as clear profit was only £3000. This seemed a very short come off after several such good years, but a careful investigation of the above figures will at once explain it as the Malt and hops alone cost fully £2000 more than the same quantities would have done in 1864 and 5. Of course the beer was not made so strong, but the difference could not any thing like be made up in that way.

This was a very fine spring and summer, but the weather was alternately very hot and then as cold for some days. At the beginning of May the heat was intense, I think as it was as hot as I ever knew it at any time in that or any other summer; then about the 13th. there was a change; it was cold and cloudy for some days and on the morning of Friday, May the 24th. there was the severest frost ever known at that time of the year. Afterwards it was occasionally very hot with refreshing showers. The harvest was a very abundant one, and the corn was all well got in. Barley was of good fair quality but dear, owing to a short stock of old Malt on hand, and the consumption was great. We bought in 1867-8, 2860 quarters at 41/7d., weight about 52 lbs. per B.

I did not do anything in real property this year except to purchase the St. Leonard's Hotel for £1000.

1868.   Brewed this year 3075 quarters of Malt at an average price of 70s. per quarter, and the cost of hops was about 6/6d. per quarter, the balance carried from Beer account to profit and loss was £7810, and from Malting £1044.

The amount carried to Capital Stock account as clear profit was £4000. This was rallying a little from last year, but we brewed the most beer we ever did in one year, but malt was so dear that it did not yield so much profit as usual. This was a very fine, hot and dry summer and Autumn. The wheat crop was very good indeed, but the barley was very inferior, in fact, there was no home grown about here and we had to rely entirely upon French, Scotch and Danish, of which we bought 3044 quarters at an average of 43/6d. per quarter, and the weight was from 53 lbs. to 55 lbs. per bushel. We did extensive repairs this year at Adversane, Billingshurst Station and B.H. Street, and several other houses and also this, now called Grandford house.

I made several small investments this year including the Beer house in Fay gate lane for £400, the Chequer at Row-hook for about £500 and the meadow attached to these premises for £525 and also 26 new shares in the Gas company.

1869.   Brewed this year 3064 quarters of Malt, 2735 quarters at 70s. and the remainder at 64s. per qr. The cost of hops was a little under 5s. per quarter, the balance carried from beer account to profit and loss was £7281 and from the malting £1002.

The Sum added to the Capital Stock account this year as clear profit was £3500, a small amount considering the amount of business done, but we sunk a good deal in repairs this year—as much as £100 at the Jolly Tanner alone— and several heavy sums from the Loan account and from Book debts, enough altogether to make up £500 more than the average.

This was a very fine summer again and the crops of corn of every description were first rate. We bought in the season 1869-70 Qrs. 3067 of barley, nearly the whole of English growth, at an average price of 37/10 per quarter and a weight of 54 to 57 lbs. per bushel.

My investments this year were £800 for Albert lodge, several small loans and about £500 laid out on the New Malthouse estate and about £1200 on Grandford house and premises.

1870.   Brewed this year 2856 quarters of Malt at 64s. per quarter, the cost of hops was 5/- per quarter, the balance carried from the Beer account to profit and loss was £7642, and from the Malting £902. The sum added to the Capital Stock account this year £4000, but this was exclusive of all rents and interest on loans as that was placed to the credit of my own private account for the first time this year, as I had arranged with my son that he should have half the profits of the business which I would not charge with any interest of money.

I ought not to have said that £4000 was added to the capital Stock this year; it is quite true that £4000 was cleared by the business, but as I had promised my Son he should have half the profit, £2000 was placed to the credit of his account and £2000 to mine, which was nearly all sunk in rebuilding, furnishing and adding land to Grandford house and premises.

This was a remarkably dry summer. There was hardly any Hay made; the meadow land generally was not mown at all. Fortunately there was a great deal of old Hay on hand (we had as much as 30 tons at Shiprods), nevertheless, it commanded a very high price, as much as from £6 to £7 per ton.

1871. Brewed this year 2677 Quarters at 65s. per qr., the cost of Hops was about 4/6 per Quarter and the balance carried from Beer to profit and Loss account was £8071, and from Malting £853.

The Amount carried from Profit and Loss to my own account was £2000, and the same to the credit of Henry Michell Junior's account.

I did not lay out much in new investments this year excepting £2000 in Victoria Bonds which were recommended to me as good security and paying Six per cent.

This was again a very fine summer, and the yield of corn was good and so was the quality.

1872. Brewed this year 2952 quarters of Malt at 64s. per quarter, the cost of Hops was 6s. per quarter. The balance carried from Beer to the profit and Loss account was £8028 and from the Malting £1016.

The Balance carried from P. & L. was £2000 to my own and the same to H.M. Junior, and my investments this year were considerable, including the purchase of property at Hand X, Bolney, Whiteman's Green, Copthorne and the Gate House, Ifield, which however, I sold again to Peter Webb.

1873. Brewed this year   quarters of Malt at 64 to 67s. per quarter, but the quality was very inferior, most of it being made from French Barley, as the supply of English and Scotch was very short and dear. The price of Hops was also more than in 1872, the cost being about 6/6 per quarter. The profit was £3600 carried to Profit and Loss, being considerably under that of the previous year, although about £2000's worth more Beer was sent out; in fact, it was the largest amount we ever returned in any one year. The profit on Malting was £734.

I renewed the Lease of the Brewery with Sir Percy Shelley this year for 14 years from Michaelmas 1872 at an advance of £25, making the rent now £250, though I had some trouble in bringing him to terms and should not probably have done so had I not threatened to Build a new Brewery on the Old Gaol ground and which I had a strong inclination to do, and I am not sure as time will not prove that it would have been the best thing for us to have done, but having renewed the Lease with Shelley, we resolved upon at once

laying out some money upon the House, which was not a
comfortable residence for our Son, and also on the Brewery
plant, and having fortunately obtained a first rate supply of
water, we added more cooling power in another of Baudelot's
cooling machines. Altogether we spent a deal of money.
We divided £1800 each as surplus of the P. and L.
account, which I added to my Capital Stock acct. but my Son
sunk the whole of his in refurnishing his House and having
been so successful in his experiment to find water in the
meadow near Tanbridge, was induced to turn the same to
account by constructing the Baths, an enterprise in which I
entirely concurred. Bought the Rudgwick house and Angleside
this year.

III

MAN OF AFFAIRS
'A Downright Radical'

That part of Henry Michell's diary which deals with his public life, reproduced at the end of this chapter, opens with a forthright declaration of his radicalism and a nice contempt for party labels. His political creed may be summed up. He was opposed to what he regarded as the reactionary elements in rural society—the squirearchy, High Church, and political nonentities among the landed nobility. He was staunchly protestant, high principled as befitted a true Victorian, liberal and 'a most decided repealer'. No one could doubt where he stood on the main issues and that at times made local political life for him uncomfortable, and it would seem, unattractive. That he wished to play his part is clear; but he seems to have had difficulty in reconciling himself to the personalities involved in local politics and, to his credit, he had no flair for political philandering. It could be said that he was uncompromising and saw the major political issues of his day in too simple terms. The dilemma was central to his political motivation and he naturally, and wisely, concentrated most of his energies on his family and business.

Henry Michell first enters the political scene in Horsham on the occasion of the by-election caused in 1844, by the elevation of the sitting member, the Hon. R. C. Scarlett, to the peerage on the death of his father. The difficulties to which I have alluded at once confronted him, but he consented to second the nomination of

R. H. Hurst, his name being coupled with that of William Lintott, the proposer and another Horsham businessman. Both he and Lintott were members of the Anti-Corn Law League.[23] Hurst, who was returned unopposed was a Protectionist and proved, as the diary shows, to be a most unsatisfactory member for the borough. One can only assume that Henry Michell subscribed to Hurst's political blank cheque on the grounds of public duty and against his better judgement. He learned to be more circumspect.

There are but a few matters on which Henry Michell waxes eloquently and with relish in the political section of the diary. The repeal of the Corn Laws was one such issue. It is the best part of the diary and reflects the political fire and public controversy that the question of repeal ignited in early Victorian England. The recent public debate about Britain's application to join the European Economic Community caused but a ripple by comparison. The Government's survival and the personal future of major politicians were at stake. At the local level society was deeply divided. The agitated gatherings at the *White Horse* in Steyning, intimidation, coercion and the strain on personal relationships during 1844-6 that this struggle provoked were etched on Henry Michell's memory and, eventually, in the diary. Some of the flavour of those hectic and stressful days lives on in his pages. 'Those great men', Cobden[24] and Bright, were his political heroes. Yet, in the end, the issue was forced by external events rather than internal pressures, and subsumed in the passage of time. Today it rates little more than a regular appearance in school examination papers. Ever was it so in the ephemeral context of political history! It is in its socio-economic aspects and in constitutional affairs that the experience of history endures. Euripedes understood this more than 2,000 years ago—'The Gods arrange many things in an unhoped-for manner . . . so fell out this affair'.

Henry Michell and his opponents would never have believed it at the time.

In his robust and somewhat petulant attitude to the landed gentry of mid-Sussex and his disillusion with the Church he is, one feels, less than fair. Most zealots are, and Henry Michell was a stickler for principle, progress and individual liberty. But, we need not seek to moderate his views about the personal obligations and qualities of Horsham's aspiring politicians. There was the disappointment with Hurst to which I have referred. The rampant corruption and notoriety that characterised the election of 1847 are here recounted and may be studied in full in William Albery's *Parliamentary History of Horsham.* The success of W. R. S. Fitzgerald in winning the support of William Lintott and Henry Michell, Horsham's 'big fish' in Albery's words, was a surprise but, in the end, it did him little good. Sir John Jervis, his opponent, won a majority of the votes but, guilty of corrupt practices was unseated and Fitzgerald dared not face the same investigation of his credentials. That Jervis, a radical Free-trader, did not secure Michell's support is something of a mystery. It appears that he opted for Fitzgerald, half-heartedly, on the strength of the latter's manifesto and, repelled by the conduct of the election, prudently stood aside. When, in 1848, the inevitable further by-election took place and Lord Edward Howard was returned following Fitzgerald's disqualification, Henry Michell would have nothing to do with it. The laconic diary entry for 1848 presages his quarrel with Lintott over Fitzgerald's candidature which he refused to support in 1852, Not until the General Election of 1865 did Henry Michell again consent to allow his name to head the list of proposers. Then it was in favour of Robert Henry Hurst of Horsham Park, the son of the successful candidate he had supported in 1844. In the meantime Fitzgerald, the Conservative candidate, who had established himself as an assiduous member for the constituency, started in a strong position and was nominated, in 1865, by William Lintott. Although anxious about his health Henry Michell made one of his rare political speeches—summarised from memory in the diary—in support of Hurst who won a narrow victory. It was robust, consistent with his political philosophy and unequivocal in its rejection of Fitzgerald's claim to the confidence of the electorate in Horsham. Hurst also won, narrowly, after a bitter election campaign, in 1868, having again been nominated by Michell. This time Henry Michell's political enthusiasms, in a short speech, were directed towards the national expenditure and the Irish Church question. Fitzgerald (by them Sir Seymour) returned to Horsham in 1874 to defeat Hurst at the first General election after the Ballot Act of 1872; Henry Michell was 'utterly astonished'. So it appears was Hurst who, at a later election, was supported by Henry Michell's son.

As part of the mechanics for promoting the interests of local political parties it was fashionable, as the electorate grew after the Reform Bill of 1867, to form local societies. The Liberal Registration Society in Horsham was founded in 1869 and Henry Michell was present as Chairman at a celebration banquet in Horsham Park. His impromptu speech was devoted to national finance and, what must have seemed largely irrelevant to his audience, the iniquities of the French monarchy on which topic he expounded at some length in his diary where he also included long extracts from the press on the same subject. These I have omitted. Conversely the Crimean War made no comparable impact upon him. It is mentioned only to note the increase it caused in the malt duty in 1854 and its reversion at the end of the war in 1855. Of the American Civil War he notes, in 1861, during a visit to the Coates factory at Paisley, that 'They were working only 2/3rds time owing to the American War'. At a chance meeting with American tourists at Lucerne in 1865 he, as one would expect, denounced the rebellion of the Southern states as 'a crime'. There is also a press extract. That is all: and the diary soon returns to the Franco-Prussian war about which he was rather obsessive. His passionate feelings about this event are not easily explained; it clearly touched a political nerve.

One public event that assumes some significance in Henry Michell's narrative and which for him clearly symbolised the entrepreneurial society to which he gladly belonged was the Great Exhibition[25] of 1851. Conceived by the Prince Consort it was an ostentatious but authentic spectacle of the Victorian economic miracle. Naturally it was the subject of some controversy but it was, nevertheless, a political and financial success. It is still of sufficient historical interest, as a manifestation of Victorian attitudes to the exciting generation of national wealth that was taking place, to justify reproducing the greater part of Henry Michell's record of the exhibition. Written as it is, from the standpoint of a local businessman, still finding his feet, and parish pump politics, we are afforded an unusual, if oblique, insight into its impact on ordinary people. William Morris's reference to what he regarded as meretricious and vulgar— 'tons and tons of unutterable rubbish'—would have shocked Henry Michell and the great majority of Victorians who did not possess the Essex craftsman's sensitive and exquisite taste.

The great international exhibition in Hyde Park was opened on the first of May this year and I never remember any great public event that was looked forward to with so much interest and anxiety, it was one of those events which marks an epoch in one's life, particularly with those who felt such a warm interest in it as we did, as calculated to promote peace on earth and goodwill towards mankind. It was not till the day before, that is April 30th, that it came into my mind to apply for season tickets which we were fortunate enough to secure through some friends in London, the price was £4 for myself and £2 for my wife, and as only season ticket holders were admitted within the great crystal palace on the opening day we were very glad to avail ourselves of so great a privilege, and we were gratified beyond anything we could have conceived: everything was so well arranged that when we reached the entrance we were immediately conducted to seats corresponding to the number of our tickets which happened to be in the galleries and an excellent view we had. The ladies were ranged on either side of the aisles on the ground floor throughout the whole length of the building, and the opening procession passed between them. First came the Queen and Prince Albert, preceded by the great officers of state walking backwards and followed by the rest of the Royal Family; then came the Duke of Wellington, the Marquis of Anglesea, foreign ambassadors, ministers of state, and of other great people, both foreign and domestic; it was indeed a grand sight and a most exalting one to see our own dear Queen and her husband, the great originator of the scene with the representatives of so many foreign countries, with whom England had often been engaged in the horrors of war, uniting to inaugurate a reign of peace, the promotion of the sciences, the expansion of commerce, and, it was hoped it would lead to the spread of the Christian religion, and as a matter of course of goodwill among men, but oh! how awfully have subsequent events proved the fallacy of this expectation.

We did not go any tour this year but made a point o devoting all the time and money we could spare in visiting the crystal palace and studying its contents with our children and all our servants and dependants at the Brewery, Farm and Brickyards, and on the 24th of September we went with all the school children in the parish to the number of 380. The movement began in this way, at one of our gas meetings Mr John Phillpot, the master of the British School said how glad his boys would be to go, and I said if they would all find 1/- each I would guarantee they should go, he made the proposition to them and I believe more than 100 out of 120 brought him their shilling. Thus encouraged I invited the co-operation of several friends in the town, including Mr John Thorpe, Mrs Redford and Miss Figg; the Vicar, Mr Hodgson, gave the movement his support, but he did not take an active practical part. My dear wife was a warm partizan and with the ladies above named and many more who interested themselves did great service in organizing the girls' schools—the total number of children was as I have stated above and comprised all those of 7 years of age and upwards in the Colleges, British and parish schools and also those in the Union house and certainly these poor children formed one of the most interesting groups of the whole party A committee was formed who met every evening at the Town

Hall and I was unanimously chosen President. I suppose I must say we at length completed our arrangements which were nearly as follows. Every child was to wear a rosette of pink, white and blue and which were provided by the Ladies and a little tin mug to every 6 or 8 with some eatables for each, each separate school was under the direction of the teachers and I was chosen General Superintendent. We went from here by special train and by steam boat (engaged for the occasion) from London Bridge to Westminster Bridge whence we marched in procession to a large tree just outside the palace and every child was instructed to come again to the same tree by 4 o'clock p.m. The police were acquainted with our arrangements and at the time and place appointed every child made his appearance when a penny bun was given to each and we returned home in the same order as we went out and I believe it was a day of great pleasure to every one concerned. I may truly say it was one of the very happiest days of my life, the very weather seemed to conspire to make it pleasant as it was a most lovely day and quite warm till we reached Horsham which was not much before 10 p.m.

Of the financial arrangements I felt so warm in the cause that I took upon myself the office of whole and sole guarantor but subscriptions flowed in so liberally that I was not left much on the wrong side.

The particulars of order of procession, the schools and costs etc: were as follows:—

ORDER OF PROCESSION

Mr Henry Michell.   Mr John Thorpe.

Mr Medwin, warden and Mr W Pirie, master of the collegers' Grammar School with the scholars	60
Mr John Tugwell and National school boys ...	47
Mr Penfold. D Southwater boys	18
Mr John Philpot and British school boys ...	130
Miss Bull and Denne school girls	70
Miss Figg and Miss Warner and British school girls	28
Union House, schoolmaster and boys	11
,, ,, ,, ,, girls	8
Attendants on the different schools	20
Making a total of	392

Instructions to leaders

To meet at the Horsham Station at 6 a.m. to follow in procession as above, to take charge of the children as allotted to them for the day and to meet at 4 p.m. in Hyde Park opposite the northern transept entrance, to return in the same order to London Bridge Station.

The whole programme was carried out to the letter and I believe that not the smallest hitch occurred anywhere. I think I should not do justice to the event without giving the financial statement in connection with it, which is as follows:—

Subscriptions from the different schools—

British	7	18	0
Denne School	3	6	0
Collyers School	3	0	0
Boys National School	2	7	0
Southwater School	1	2	0
Inhabitants by collectors	42	9	6
	60	2	6
Balance by myself	3	13	8
	63	16	2

Railway special train	38	7	0				
Entrance to Crystal Palace	18	18	0				
Steamboat from London to Westminster Bridge and return	3	9	0				
Buns for children	1	0	8				
I Phillpot	1	0	0				
Sundries		10	6	63	16	2	

The Railway Company charged at the rate of 2/6 for every child over 10 years of age and 1/6 for all under, for the journey to London Bridge and return, which the committee considered very liberal indeed and they were highly gratified with their cooperation altogether.

I think now I have said all I know of this great affair for such it seemed to be at any rate at the outset.

When we first came to Horsham the Town, I remember was considered highly favoured in having a coach to London by which one might for 14/- and 2/- the driver, go there and back between the hours of 7a.m. and 8 p.m. and have about 4 hours there; well then might it be thought a great undertaking to take nearly 400 children there for a regular day's pleasure. Ah! indeed all who have lived to see and feel the advantages of Railway communication must feel, if they think at all on the subject that they have lived to see and participate in very great privileges and I am sorry to say very often at the cost of the unfortunate shareholders.

I shall conclude this subject by saying that I sincerely hope if ever a similar opportunity should offer for my children or grandchildren to promote the pleasure and happiness of the children of their poorer brethren they will not fail to do so, as such acts certainly bring a considerable reward, even in this life. I can safely affirm that I never think of the 24 of September 1851 but with the greatest pleasure and satisfaction.

When it came to the further exhibition in 1862 Henry Michell was less enthusiastic:

1862. This year was again celebrated for its great international exhibition. It was opened as before (in 1851) on the 1st. of May. The first entry I find in my accounts relative to it is on the 10th. of April,—Exhibition tickets £15. 15. 0, which was for season tickets for all four of us. We went up on the opening day, but of course there was not that charm of novelty about it which there was in 1851, nor was the building itself of that extraordinary character, but still it was altogether very interesting. The building and its contents were, I should say, as varied and extensive as in 1851. The opening was celebrated as nearly as possible in the same way, but was not graced by the presence of the Queen in consequence of the lamented death of Prince Albert on the 13th. of December 1861. Nevertheless, all the great officers of state were there, as well as many members of our Royal family, and the crown prince of Prussia and all the other foreign Ambassadors. It was a very grand and imposing ceremony, and we returned home highly gratified, and in order to acquaint ourselves as soon as possible with some idea of the whole thing, we went up again on the second (the next day) and I believe we paid as many as 14 visits during the summer by ourselves, without reckoning those with our men from the Brewery, Farm, and Brickyards, with their families as much as practicable, and I need hardly say that we were all highly gratified. The only one thing to embitter one's reflections on it was that the good prince Albert did not live to see his own conceptions of World wide philanthropy carried to such a degree of maturity and success.

Among the other topics in which Michell was sufficiently interested to include extracts from reported speeches were the national economy, agricultural cottages, church services and ritual, and the historic meeting of Stanley and Livingstone at Ujiji in 1871.[26]

In 1843, Henry Michell, whose views upon church matters were equally as strong and radical as his political opinions, came into conflict with the local clergy. At the time he was churchwarden at St. Mary's, Horsham and John Fisher Hodgson, the vicar, was, according to Michell, a follower of Edward Pusey[27] whose views Michell repudiated with feeling. There was an altercation over the church collection, pew by pew as is normal now, which, hitherto, had relied on the muted appeal of a suitable plate placed discreetly at the church door for the convenience of the departing parishioners. A piquant correspondence followed between Henry Michell and the curate, James Kenrick, which later involved the vicar[28] and the Bishop of Chichester. The essence of this correspondence was the drift, at Horsham's parish churches, towards 'false doctrine' and opposition to liturgical change. Henry Michell led a meeting of church members at which a resolution condemning the changes was passed unanimously and transmitted to the Bishop. He, for his part, replied in somewhat neutral terms, urging the parishioners to offer due deference and affection to their clergy. The matter could not rest there and Henry Michell and about 40 other parishioners submitted a long address to the vicar:

To The Reverend John Fisher Hodgson,
     Vicar of the Parish of Horsham.

We the undersigned parishioners of Horsham being members of the protestant established Church of England feel most reluctantly constrained by a deep and overwhelming sense of duty to ourselves our fellow parishioners and our Church to which we have the happiness to belong, to address you in the language of complaint and respectful remonstrance in refference to the mode in which the rites and services of the Church, are at this time administered and conducted in this parish.

It is with infinite pain and regret that we have witnessed the numerous alterations and innovations which have been from time to time introduced by yourself, or with your sanction in the mode of conducting the services of the Churches in this Parish, but more especially in that of St. Marks.

Such novelties and frequent changes during the celebration of Divine service necessarily have the effect of unsettling and disturbing the minds, and distracting the thoughts of the congregations and are therefore injurious under any circumstances but in the present state of the Church in this Kingdom, and threatened as it is with dangers from within and without any change whatever in the accustomed services and ceremonies of the Church becomes an evil of fearful magnitude and cannot fail to excite feelings of apprehension in all who feel interested in maintaining our revered protestant Church in its integrity, such feelings alone are entitled to and must we think you will admit, command the respect and consideration of every faithful minister, who weighs well the great responsibility he undertakes in accepting the spiritual charge of a large flock.

We feel deeply however the innovations and changes of which we complain, are in themselves of a highly objectionable character, and calculated, if acquiesced in, seriously to injure the true interests of the Church, and to become precedents for still further alterations at a future period. The objectionable practices and innovations in this Parish in common with many other parishes (in some of which we have the satisfaction of knowing that the Clergymen have since discontinued them in deference to the wishes of the inhabitants) are adopted in accordance with the views advocated in certain well known writings of a dangerous and mischievous character emanating from Oxford University, which have been publicly condemned not only by the Heads of the University but by high authoritys in the Church. In these writings principles directly opposed to the principles of the reformation are asserted, the Reformation itself condemned, the very name of protestant repudiated and a closer approximation of the English Church, to the corrupted Church of Rome ardently and openly advocated. Of the principal Authors of these writings the most distinguished (whose works have been constantly quoted by yourself and recommended to members of your Flock has recently publicly abjured the Church of England and entered the Church of Rome, another scarcely less eminent has been publicly suspended from the performance of his high functions as a teacher in the University of

Oxford for the dessemination of erroneous and heretical Doctrines and others have also openly left the Church of England and entered the Church of Rome; and it was with infinite mortification and pain we learned that the Pastors of our two Churches were found among the number of those who attended at Oxford to screen, but happily without success, a Clergyman of the English Protestant Church, who openly avowed Romish doctrines, from being expelled that university.

It is not therefore without well grounded feelings of apprehension and dismay that we have seen practices of ceremonies introduced into our Churches and constantly recurring novelties in the celebration of Divine Worship all of which progress in the direction previously travelled by those Clergymen who have since entered the Romish Church, and but too often have carried with them many of their Flocks.

In our own parish one most lamentable effect has resulted from these changes; when you, Sir, took the charge of this Parish, you found the Parish Church crowded, and, in consequence of the want of sufficient accommodation therein for the parishioners a new Church was in course of erection to supply the deficiency. The greatest unanimity, harmony, and enthusiasm prevailed among the members of the Church and on the retirement of your respected predecessor, The Rev. W. H. Simpson, you were when introduced by him, received with a hearty welcome, which you can hardly forget, and which continued as long as Divine Worship was conducted in the way to which the people had been accustomed.

Contrast this state of things with that which has existed since the Church services have been changed, and you find that the congregations have gradually decreased, until at this (?) the greatest apathy and indifference is manifested on the part of the greater number of your Flock and dissatisfaction with their clergyman universally prevails.

We deem it therefore our imperative duty respectfully but energetically to protest against the several changes which you have had in the celebration of Divine Worship and to request that you will comply with the earnest wishes of your parishioners and restore the Church services to that plain simple and efficient state in which they were conducted by your predecessors The Revd. W. H. Simpson and the Revd. Hugh James Rose.

Signed by about 40 members of the congregations.

It all ended in anti-climax. Henry Michell writes, ruefully, rejecting the

> idea that the Churchwardens could control the clergy in the celebration of divine service, but the records of the Ecclesiastical courts will show the utter delusion of such a notion; the costs alone are a complete bar to any proceedings being taken there by any ordinary man.

He played therefore, a fairly active, but not significant part in local affairs. That he was politically minded is evident, but it was usually in national and international affairs that his interest lay. Horsham's local issues did not excite his civic conscience to any great extent. Indeed he had a mild cynicism, born of experience and the natural instincts of a thrusting and successful man. In the last year of his life, in despair at local apathy and ineptitude he wrote:

> I am fully convinced that of Horsham it may be said that if you wish to do anything to benefit the people, you must find some way of doing it in spite of themselves.

That sentence alone illustrates the basic change that has taken place in social attitudes and the quality of life in the town since Henry Michell died a hundred years ago. In the pages of his diary that now follow, we are introduced to a very different world. It is one that Henry Michell has, in a modest way, helped us to understand:

> I believe I may say I was always considered by my own family and friends as something more than a liberal in politics, nay, even a downright radical. However that may be, I always stoutly maintained that I was a downright conservative and for this reason I maintain that the terms Whig, Tory, or radical are merely party definitions, whereas conservatism signifies a principal, the principal of advocating the greatest good to the greatest number; upon this ground I have always held that such men as Richard Cobden and John Bright are in reality the great conservative leaders of the party of progress, notwithstanding their denunciation by our country squires, political nobodies, and Lords Dundreary, as demagogues, radicals, and dangerous characters. Bright and Cobden always in reply to their political opponents said that what was called the Radicalism of to-day proved the conservatism of the future,

and the course of events fully proved they were right. I remember well the agitation for the abolition of slavery, the Catholic emancipation bill, the reform bill of 1832, the repeal of the corn laws, and many other demonstrations of a like character; to every one of these measures the Tory party, headed by the church, offered an uncompromising opposition, and in all country districts where the parson and the squire are paramount, any one who dares to advocate any one of these measures was made to feel the weight of their displeasure.

I remember about the year '27 or '28 at any rate, it was only just a year or two before the abolition of slavery, there was a meeting got up at the White horse at Steyning for the purpose of adopting a petition to Parliament in its favour. The room was crowded and the meeting was most enthusiastic in support of the petition. The only opposition offered to it was by the Rev. John Evans and John Tribe a lawyer, true to their cloth: but their resistance was hooted down in a most uproarious manner, and they were near being turned out of the room.

1835.   The agitation for the repeal of the corn laws began to assume a very decided form just as we came to Horsham and so far as my humble position would allow me, I entered the lists as a most decided repealer, which often placed me in a most unpleasant position with my nearest and dearest friends, but I felt so warmly in the cause that I don't believe I ever sacrificed my principles to expediency. I knew the only hope lay in the domination of the Whig party and the corn laws was the great question of the day when a vacancy occurred in the representation of Horsham in 1844.

1844.   Mr. Robert Hy. Hurst offered himself as a candidate and I was asked to second his nomination, and I did so. There was no opposition to Mr. Hurst, and therefore he was returned as a matter of course. He soon, however, fell into pecuniary embarrassment and very seldom appeared in the house of Commons. He, however, recorded his vote against corn law repeal. His agent, Mr. Padwick, and myself had several rather acrimonious discussions on this subject which I wound up by declaring that with Free trade England would be to the World what London is to England, and that as to depreciation of Land, it would all be wanted for pleasure grounds and cabbage gardens, and experience has proved that my assertion, though made somewhat at random, had some truth in it. The 'Times' in speaking of this election stated 'Mr. Hurst was nominated by a Mr. Lintott, a Free trader, and was seconded by Mr. Henry Michell, another Free trader'. O, how often have I felt proud of this reproach, for such it was intended to be.

Just about this time the agitation for the repeal of the corn laws began to assume a most violent character. Meetings were held all over the country to which tenant farmers were driven by notice from the landlords' agents, and the poor agricultural labourer was coaxed and persuaded to attend, and it was attempted to make them believe that dear bread was a good thing for them, upon the hypothesis that the more prosperous the Farmers were, the better it must be for the labourers. But it would not do. The fallacy of protection had taken too deep root in the public mind, and was doomed to fall, though not without a desperate struggle carried on as above stated.

I remember a meeting being held in the Swan field in a booth. The weather was very cold. I did not attend, as I feared I might commit myself, but the proceedings were of the most tame and uninteresting character. I went into the market room afterwards and the Farmers were loudly advocating exclusive dealing in favour of course of their supporters. Cobden and Bright were denounced as the worst characters that ever existed; they were accused of revolutionizing the country. The repeal of the corn laws, they said, must subvert the monarchy and sever Church and State, and I was pointedly appealed to if such would not be the result. I have my own views upon such points which I did not think proper to enter upon then and there, but I merely said in reply that I would defy any gentleman present to produce any statement evolving any political principle ever made by Bright or Cobden, but its object and tendency was 'the greatest good for the greatest number'. No reply was made to this, and I believe nothing more was said upon the subject.

1846.   In the early part of 1846 I was at Steyning quite accidentally, and there was a protectionist meeting at the White horse in the market room. I went with the crowd and after hearing the usual amount of stuff about Free trade being the ruin of the country and that Parliament ought to be urged to throw out or set aside the measure, the question was put that all who were of this opinion should hold up

their hands. A good many were held up, but a good many
were not, and when the question was put that those who
were of a contrary opinion should hold up theirs, I immediately held up mine, supposing that many others would do
the same, but to my surprise mine was the only one, which
provoked roars of laughter. I, indeed, I pitied them, but to
shew how seriously some people thought of the affair, Sir C.
Burrell—poor old simpleton—met me at Petworth a few days
after and said how sorry he was for the part I had acted at the
Steyning meeting, that the present was a most serious crisis
in the country, and that we ought to be unanimous in support
of protection to native industry. I did not deign any reply,
as I considered my opinion as good as his, and it very soon
proved a good deal better.

I think it was in 1845 that my wife and myself attended
the great Free trade Bazaar in Covent garden theatre. This
great struggle was now approaching the culminating point
when the famine in Ireland suddenly opened the eyes of
many of our leading statesmen headed by Sir Robert Peel,
who now saw that the cause of free trade as advocated by
those great men, Bright and Cobden, was no other than the
cause of truth and justice, and the iniquitous old system of
protection was very soon abolished, though not without a
severe struggle for its retention by all the parsons, Burrells[29]
and Gorings[30] in the Kingdom, but it was no use.

1847.   Mr. Hurst sat for Horsham from 1844 to the dissolution of Parliament this year, when there was a general election
and as the free trade question was settled in which leading men
of both sides had been so much occupied, that there really
seemed to be no great political question cropping up to which
men could attach themselves by any party distinction. The
consequence was that men offered themselves upon the most
ambiguous principles and though it was evident the new
system of commercial legislation just entered upon must
necessitate great and sweeping changes in our whole fiscal
system, it was also evident that in consequence of the course
taken by Sir Robert Peel, the leader of the Tory party, there
had been such a complete disruption of parties, that it was
very difficult to know what party a candidate belonged to
from his address 'to the free and independent electors' whom
he aspired to represent in parliament.

W. R. S. Fitzgerald of Holbrook offered himself for
Horsham and as his address seemed to offer all that could
be expected under the circumstances, I promised him my

support before there was any other candidate in the field. Subsequently a son of Sir J. Jervis came out, and there was a long and bitter contest in which bribery, drinking and corruption ran rampant, but I always steered clear of such matters and would have nothing to do with it, beyond what I could do in what I conceived quite a legitimate way, and subsequently I had abundant cause to be thankful I adopted this course. Mr. Fitzgerald was returned by a very small majority, but was unseated by petition from Jervis's party, and many of Mr. Fitzgerald's friends very nearly got into trouble under the operation of the 'corrupt practices at Elections bill' as it was called.

1848.   The result of this was that there was another election, when Lord Edward Howard came forward to oppose Mr. Fitzgerald, who again offered himself, but it ended in the return of Lord E. Howard as Mr. Fitzgerald was declared ineligible. After this there was a complete lull in political and party strife here till the general election of 1852 and throughout the country all parties seemed pretty quiet. The liberals were satisfied with their triumphs in free trade and the Tories from a sense of submission to the powers that be.

1852.   There was a general election this year and its object seemed to be an attempt on the part of the Tories to return to the exploded system of protection, and there were very many who really persuaded themselves that that was the only way of, as they said, of saving the country; a very pretty way, certainly, to save a country, to starve it. Lord Palmerston at this time became very unpopular from truckling in some way to the Emperor of the French, and his government fell to pieces upon this. Lord Derby was made prime minister and the tory party flattered themselves that from this cause and the malcontent on Free trade they should come into power with an overwhelming majority in the general election and be enabled to carry matters with a high hand. Mr. Fitzgerald again offered himself for Horsham and was returned without opposition. Lord Derby and his party were completely discomfited. As soon as ever the result of the general election was correctly ascertained, he hastened to Osborne house to tender his resignation to the Queen and, singularly enough we, that is, myself wife and children, were in Southampton Docks when he was on his way there, and we had a good view of him as he went down the dock stairs and on board the despatch boat which was waiting for him. Poor man, I quite pitied him, as the hopes and aspirations of his party I believe much more than himself were utterly unfounded, and there was not the least chance of the Tory programme being adopted by the country.

But my object is not to write, even if I had the means at command and the ability to carry it out, the political history of my country, but only to record such facts and circumstances as had an influence upon myself or me upon them, so far as my humble means would avail. I recollect when Mr. Fitzgerald offered himself at this time (1852) I was assured his address would be such as the most liberal could not quarrel with, and Mr. W. Lintott, with whom I had often acted in political matters up to this period, asked me to meet him at his house to discuss the address together. I had just read it over when Mr. Fitzgerald asked me my opinion upon it. I at once told him I could not support him. Mr. Lintott poured out some wine and proposed his (Mr. Fitzgerald's) health and success, upon which I got up and left the room and Mr. Lintott and myself never acted in concert afterwards upon political matters and I have never had reason to regret this decisive step on my part, as Mr. Fitzgerald's subsequent acts proved that I had rightly estimated his views as being antagonistic to all progress. However, as there was no other candidate in the field, he was returned without opposition and political matters settled down very quietly and every one seemed to forget that Horsham was a borough Town. This is as it should be, and I believe as it would be, were it not for the electioneering agents and the Clergy.

1857.   There was a general election this year, as parliament had run its course, and Mr. Scott offered himself for Horsham, but he made no great effort to be returned. I never heard of his having any committee even, and I believe his object was to test the strength of the liberal party. I voted for him early in the morning and I have every reason to believe my doing so brought him several more votes. At the close of the poll the numbers were Fitzgerald 172, Scott 117. I believe Mr. Scott polled as many votes as he expected under the circumstances. This election was extremely well conducted. There was no Band, no favours, no open public houses, and the whole affair was a credit to both parties. Anyone would hardly have known that an election was going on in the town. It must be borne in mind there was no great leading political question agitating just now. Free trade had proved such a boon to the nation that no one save here and there one of the old school of the Burrell or Richmond type had a word to say against it.

1859. In March this year Lord Derby's government being beaten on their reform bill, parliament was dissolved and an election took place in April. The New parliament met on the 31st of May; the amendment to the address was carried against the government. On this Lord Derby resigned and Lord Palmerston was again Premier. At this election in Horsham no opposition can be said to have been offered to the return of Mr. Fitzgerald, though a person calling himself* made his appearance in the town, but as no one knew anything of him and he could get little or no support, he took himself off again. I was asked to meet him at the Anchor, but I never would take a lead in election matters and refused to support him in any way, excepting that I would vote for him if he came to the poll and I was satisfied of his bona fides.

1865. From the last general election in 1859 to this present year the political atmosphere was again undisturbed by any great excitement excepting by rumours of reform in parliament, and I believe the great question referred to the constituencies was not whether there was to be a reform bill at all, but whether it was to be carried by Whigs or Tories. A dissolution of parliament took place and a general election ensued. I was in Switzerland when the contest may be said to have begun here, and very glad I was to be out of the way. Mr. Hurst came forward in the liberal interest and Mr. Fitzgerald in the Tory. I had no hesitation at all in giving my warm support to Mr. Hurst, who asked me to nominate him. I thanked him for the compliment and said I would most willingly do so if I was able, but I feared I should break down in the attempt, as I was very unwell and had been ever since we walked from Chamounix to the Montauvert on Saturday, June 17, which was registered as one of the hottest days ever known. I did not feel it at all at the time, but a few days after I was quite ill. We reached Paris on Friday the 23rd. and I could get no further. We put up at the Hotel Meurice, where we remained till the following Monday, when I was well enough to start again and we reached home the following day. I soon found myself in the heat of election matters, but I did not mix myself up with them at all, excepting to assist

*A. J. Roberts.

Mr. Hurst in the nomination as before stated, which took place on the 11th. of July. I was sadly afraid I should make a mess of it, and yet I felt so warmly on the Subject that I had a strong hope I should get through it pretty well, and the reason of my hope was this, that every liberal measure affecting the commercial interests of the Nation and which the Liberals had always advocated, had become Law and had culminated in a degree of prosperity hitherto without a parallel: here was a theme to dwell upon, one upon which I felt that had I but the gift of a ready writer, I could fill volumes, but how to make a short telling speech to a mob (and I had anticipated a howling mob) that was the thing. But to my utter astonishment when I came to the front to speak, all was still and orderly. I must say I never felt such a momentary relief. I looked upon it as an act of homage to the political principles it was well known I had always held, and feeling strong in the justice of my cause, I delivered myself as nearly as I can recollect of the following words:

Gentlemen Electors of the Borough of Horsham.

I beg to propose Robert Henry Hurst Esq. of Horsham Park as a fit and proper person to represent this Borough in Parliament. Brother Electors

I have lived among you now for about Thirty years and I can very well understand your asking me, as you have a good right to do, why I think Mr. Hurst is the right man for us as member. Well then, I will tell you why I think so. If you look back for the last twenty years you will find that the Liberal party headed, I may say, by that great man Richard Cobden, and with Lord Palmerston at the head of the government have succeeded in enacting a succession of Laws which have had the effect of raising our country to an unparalleled degree of prosperity and Mr. Hurst has promised that, if he is elected, he will give his support to the liberal party, and I think that is of itself a very good reason why we should all think him a fit person to be our member. Another reason why I think so, is that if you look at Mr. Hurst as a fellow Townsman, he is always at his post to do any good he can for us, indeed I may sum up by saying that as a neighbour, a magistrate, a gentleman, and in every relation of life his character is irreproachable. Having said thus much as to why you ought to vote for Mr. Hurst, I will venture to tell you why you ought to vote against Mr. Fitzgerald, and I say the reason why is that Mr. Fitzgerald and his party have done all they could to oppose Free trade and every kindred measure, which it has been proved has been so beneficial to the country, and we have no reason to believe they will do otherwise in the future, and therefore I think that is ample reason why you should vote against him.

Brother Electors come then early to the poll to-morrow and prove by an overwhelming majority that Mr. Fitzgerald and his Friends with their retrograde policy will not be accepted by the Borough of Horsham. I thank you for your kind attention.

I did thank them from the very bottom of my heart as I thought their kindness to me arose partly out of sympathy for me, from having been so unwell. As a proof of this, Mr. Stott, the manager of Henty's Bank, told me he did not know me at first I was so altered. My fears as to my being able to bear up under the excitement were not altogether groundless, as I had retired to the back of the Hustings only a very few minutes before I was taken ill with a fainting fit. My doctor happened to be on the Hustings; he attended me at once. I was poorly for a few days when I recovered my usual state of health. I will add that Mr. Hurst, his Father in law (Mr. Scott) and many more congratulated me most warmly on my speech. I am bound to say that with all its defects it certainly was better than I had expected of myself.

The poll took place next day, when the numbers were Mr. Hurst 164, Mr. Fitzgerald 159; majority for Mr. Hurst 5. A petition was presented against Mr. Hurst's return, but it failed utterly and Mr. Hurst was declared duly elected.

I have said nothing here of what other parties said on the Hustings as my object is simply to record my own political doings, but as Mr. Fitzgerald paid me the compliment to allude to me in his speech, I think I ought to mention it, it was this. 'Mr. Michell has told you you ought to vote for Mr. Hurst because the liberals have always advocated Free trade, and every similar measure. Why, as to that, Free trade is now the great and accepted principle of the commercial legislation of this country and no one would think of contro-verting it??!!!' My dear readers, whoever you may be, I beg you will pause here for a moment and weigh the bearing of these words upon myself. Here is a man, a statesman, a 'right honourable', a privy councillor, and now governor of Bombay, indirectly compelled by force of circumstances over which he had no control to declare in the face of assembled Horsham that he had always been wrong and consequently that I had been right, and this leads me to

a review of the many leading measures which have been
enacted by the House of Commons since I had taken an
interest in politics such as the abolition of slavery and the
emancipation of the slaves, the removal of many degrading
laws against the nonconformists to the Church of England,
the reform act of 1832, the repeal of the corn and navigation
laws, and even cheap postage. Then there is the disestablishment of the Irish Church, and the revision of the Tariff of
duties on imports and exports and the repeal of the duties
on Bricks, on Beer, paper, Glass, Leather, and a complete
simplification of the whole system of National taxation which
has caused an expansion and development of Trade far exceed-
ing anything the most sanguine could have anticipated; as one
instance of this I will mention a fact in the Brick trade. In
1841 the census shows that 45,000 people were employed
in the manufacture of Bricks. The duty was repealed about
1847 or 1848, and in the next census of 1851 it is shown that
95,000 were so employed and a similar result has occurred
in every department of trade and manufacture, and all these
wonderful benefits, as they have proved to be, were
obtained against the strenuous and determined hostility
of a party who call themselves conservatives. I can understand
why Landowners, Shipowners, Farmers, and many kinds of
trade and manufactures should, from ignorance of the operations of free trade fancy each in their individual interests
would be made to suffer from the change, but why ever the
clergy should be always found in the ranks opposed to all
progress is past my comprehension as it is so palpable that
restricted employment must conduce to low living, and a
deterioration of the physical and moral condition of the
working classes, than which nothing can render them more
impervious to any good influence from the spiritual minis-
trations of the Church; and here I think I may very properly
say a few words on the law of settltement. This Law, which
is even now (1871) pretty nearly forgotten, has been repealed
but a few years, and I have no doubt but many will wonder
what it was, and what were its effects upon the working
man. I will describe it as concisely as I can. A claimant for
Parish relief as aid from the poor rate was called, was bound
to apply to the parish to which he belonged, and by law he
belonged to the parish in which he resided, unless the Officers
of the same could prove he belonged elsewhere. There were
2 ways of gaining a settlement in a parish—the one was by
birth, and the other so many years residence. This led to
very short time contracts between Master and man and to
the doing away with as many cottages as possible, in all small

parishes, or in those where the lands were in the power of a few owners. The effect of this system was most grievous. The poor were driven off the land, and crowded together in adjacent villages, Towns and Hamlets and were compelled to walk several miles to and from their work daily. It is utterly impossible to overestimate the baneful effects which must arise from such a state of things to the social, moral and physical condition of the people subject to them and which at last happily led to all but a total abolition of the Law of Settlement and consequently to the erection by Land-owners of comfortable cottages on their Estates, at least this was the result in many instances, to my own knowledge.

1868. The great political questions of the day were a new reform bill and the Irish Church. Mr. Gladston was at the head of the Government with an overwhelming majority; he very soon brought in a bill extending the Franchise to house-hold suffrage, but by first one trick and then another on the part of the Tory party the reform act as at present constituted, was not passed till the summer of 1868.

A general election ensued in November. Mr. Hurst and Major Aldridge offered themselves for Horsham; party spirit ran very high, the Tory party were very sore at having been compelled by force of public opinion to help in carrying the extension of the Suffrage to Householders as well at their strong opposition to the disestablishment of the Irish Church and other liberal measures it was well known Mr. Gladston had on his mind. The contest was very bitter indeed and ended in a double return, but on a scrutiny of votes several of Major Aldridge's were proved to be bad, indeed they had no right to have been on the register at all, and it ended by a declaration in Mr. Hurst's favour by 8 votes.

Upon this occasion I was again pressed to nominate Mr. Hurst, but having delivered myself so satisfactorily in 1865 upon the subject of Free trade, I thought it would not do to harp upon the same string again, and therefore I felt myself at sea, but considering the national expenditure and the Irish Church question as two of the most prominent subjects for discussion, I said a few words on each, but I must say not at all to my satisfaction; but there was such an uproar that it did not matter much what any one said, which I was very glad of.

From this time political feeling was very quiet in the town of Horsham for several years, each party gave their supporters

a dinner which they termed a Banquet (save the mark). Mr.
Hurst's party dined in tents in Horsham Park on the 28th of
June 1869. Mr. White, M.P. for Brighton, and several other
Members were present, not many neighbouring gentry, but
Mr. Henry Broadwood of Lyne, Mr. Pigot and a few others
were there. Of course among other toasts. that of the
'Horsham Liberal registration Association' was given with
my name as Chairman of the same, and consequently I had
to return thanks and of course to make a speech, which put
me out very much as I had not expected it, and was, beside,
not at all well. However, previous speakers had alluded to a
subject always in my mind as one of the greatest national
questions of the day, that is, our enormous national expenditure and the tendency of the Tory party to increase rather
than diminish the same. This gave me an opportunity of
speaking upon the reckless expenditure of this country during
the 25 years war, ending with the battle of Waterloo in 1815,
a subject which I have never been able to dwell upon with
common patience, and upon this occasion I believe I waxed
warm even to intemperance. I alleged that we were now paying
26 millions a year interest on the national debt, nearly the
whole of which was incurred for no other purpose than to
reinstate the Bourbon family on the throne of France in
opposition to the Buonapartes, especially to Napoleon the 1st.,
and yet what do we see at this present time? Why, many of
the monarchs of Europe who urged England on in this mad
career have passed altogether into oblivion, and notwithstanding that rivers of blood were shed, and mountains of gold
was spent, we now see a nephew of the first Napoleon on the
Throne of France and the remains of the latter reclaimed
from exile and reposing beneath such a mausoleum as few
earthly potentates are honored with. It was only in May 1868
that I (with Mrs. Michell, Mrs. Cowan and Mary Ellis were
in Paris and) paid a visit to Napoleon's tomb in the 'Hotel
des Invalid' and a most imposing structure altogether it is,
and a withering memento upon the folly of our Forefathers
in meddling with the political and Dynastic quarrels of other
nations. I congratulate my brother Electors on our success
at the last Election, although all the Clergy, professional
men, parish officials, Magistrates and indeed all the powers
that be were ranged against us, and I urged upon them the
necessity of each one attending to the registration on behalf
of himself and others who might need stimulation.

1870. It is certainly very singular that I should have made
such an allusion as I did to the Buonapartes, to their assumption

of power in spite of the opposition of powerful monarchies, since passed away; little did I then think the Dynasty of the Buonapartes was so near its fall. It was on the following 15th. of July that France declared War against Prussia. I at once saw the madness of it and from what I have seen of both Nations (which I admit was very little) I was convinced that France was no match for Prussia and stated my conviction in the presence of several people in our reading room, and added that I had no doubt but Napoleon would be defeated and that if he survived to return to Paris at all, it would be to be hurled from his throne by his own people. On the 4th. of September Napoleon 3rd. surrendered to the King of Prussia at Sedan. Eugenia fled ignominiously from Paris, and both subsequently found an asylum in England, where I am sorry to say they meet with a great deal more sympathy than they deserve, as I cannot understand upon what possible ground any one can justify a man who, from motives of ambition and for the aggrandizement of himself and his own family plunged his great nation into all the horrors of War which involved in one country (France) not only the loss of hundreds of thousands of lives, but a loss of hundreds of millions of money to the impoverishment of the present and many future generations, and in Germany the loss of many thousand lives beside founding a deep rooted hatred between 2 great and enlightened nations, which it is only too probable may prove the seeds of future Wars; and as for my own feeling towards Napoleon, I am sorry for anyone's misfortunes, but I believe he richly deserved the fall he met with, and think it's a great pity that him and his son, and indeed every member of the family had not been sacrificed on the field of Battle with those they had compelled to take part (and no doubt in most cases against their own will) in the strife. Can any one read the history of Europe from the commencement of this century to the present time and come to any other conclusion?

1871. After the fall of Napoleon at Sedan, the French declared for a Republican government who refused the terms of peace offered by the King of Prussia. Then came the Siege of Paris with all its horrors, which terminated about February this year, the French being completely conquered, and were obliged to subject themselves to very hard terms imposed by their enemies, but not any too hard, excepting that the innocent suffer alike with the guilty.

As to Home politics, the Liberal party seemed firmly seated in power and carried every Session many great and useful measures, and above all in consequence of the great and increasing prosperity of the country, were enabled to reduce the income, and many other taxes, including the simplification of the assessed taxes, which before were very vexatious and complicated. It is needless to say, that all these reforms and great beneficial measures received as usual all the opposition the Tory party could possibly bring to bear, but the most flagrant piece of extravagance we heard of of late years was the management of the Abissynian War. As to the justice of this war I believe the less said the better. When Mr. Disraeli first brought the subject before parliament, he stated the reasons why it had been resolved upon and that the estimated cost was certainly that it would not exceed three millions of money, but it lingered, and the costs kept increasing till they amounted to nine millions, an excess over the estimates which I believe never was satisfactorily cleared up, although a commission was appointed to enquire into it. Mr. Fitzgerald was appointed governor of Bombay soon after he lost his election here in 1865, and as such had a good deal to do with organizing the despatch of troops etc. from Bombay to Abissynia, and it is considered he was very extravagant in his arrangements; at all events, he left Bombay at the end of his term of Office (5 years) without any eclat; in fact the 'Times' said of him, 'that he left no doubt some personal friends behind him, but his political call was hateful to the people there'.

During the early part of this year there was great danger of our being involved in War, as the sympathies of the Tories were with the French, for no other reason than that the Germans were proving themselves too great a people, and our Warmongers pretended that as there was now no danger to be apprehended from a French invasion, and the Germans as a united people must feel their power to be irresistable, it must be necessary to let them know that nevertheless they had better be civil to us; in fact the War party in England did every thing which insult could do to provoke the ill will of the German people, but Mr. Gladston's government steered the vessel of State through all the many complications arising from a war between two such great and near neighbours as France and the German States, to all their neighbours.

1872. This year was particularly quiet in Horsham. The Liberal party were carrying out their great programme in parliament, which however being anticipated by the country at large caused no surprise or sensation. The Horsham people were looking forward to Mr. Fitzgerald's return, which did not occur till the summer of 1873, and many were the speculations as to the cause of the delay.

1873. However, there was at once a meeting of the Tory party here, and Major Aldridge resigned the leadership in favour of Fitzgerald, and it was known there must be a general Election before long, so all parties were on the watch for an opportunity to further their own cause and as the Ballot act has recently been passed there was much speculation as to how it would operate. I must admit that I always thought it would, with Household suffrage, work in favour of the Liberal party, but I was mistaken, and so I believe was the country at large.

Mr. Gladston's Government had carried many great and important measures affecting the Church and Land, in Ireland, the Army and Navy by economy, the Licensing system, Sanitary Laws and many more changes, (which though urged by public opinion) and especially general education, had in their individual effect, no doubt caused loss and inconvenience to some parties and which there is no doubt when combined to overthrow the government was really sufficient for the purpose. The clergy and many staunch Church people were in fear for the English Church, the Military were dissatisfied with arrangements for the abolition of purchase, the Navy, and Dock yard Towns did not like the economy of Mr. Gladston's administration, the Publicans almost universally rebelled against the new Licensing Laws, and the Bible clauses of the Education act[31] offended many protestant dissenters, as well as church people; with all these elements of disaffection Mr. Gladston's Government resolved not to meet the then existing parliament again, although they had an undoubted majority of 66, but it was 120 on the first assembling of the new parliament after the general election in November 1868, so a dissolution was resolved upon, and a general election took place in February 1874 and the result was a majority for the Tories of 50, which I believe astonished the whole country.

1874. The strongholds of Radicalism, such as Brighton and many other places which had always before returned Liberals, almost, without exception, returned not only conservatives, but down right Tories and there is no doubt but very many of these results was caused almost entirely by a combination of the Licensed Victuallers acting in obedience to directions from the 'Licensed Victuallers Association'. There never was anything more unjust altogether, as no doubt all the acts of the Liberal government were framed upon the principle of the greatest good to the greatest number, and were called for by the country.

As to Horsham the constituency had increased about 200 since 1868, nearly the whole of whom it would seem voted for Fitzgerald, at any rate the numbers were 529 for him and 311* for Mr. Hurst, a result at which I was utterly astonished, as looking at the two men in any relation of life there can be no doubt as to who Horsham ought to have chosen, but the whole aristocratic influence of the neighbourhood, together with nearly all the Victualling interest (and many dissenters joined them upon some religious dogma) so that it is perhaps no wonder it ended as it did. It at all events is no wonder that we are tempted sometimes to despair of doing any good, as I am fully convinced that of Horsham it may be said that if you wish to do anything to benefit the people, you must find some way of doing it in spite of themselves.

There is no doubt but the Tory party owed their majority to other causes beside those I have before stated. The late Government in carrying many of their measures did not act sufficiently on the Democratic principle to please the Ultra radicals and so they to avenge themselves returned Tories. There is no doubt also that the strikes and Unions among the Artizan, Mining and Labouring classes was creating a good deal of alarm in the country, and induced a great many timid people to join the Tory party as farthest removed from the chances of too great and revolutionary changes.

*329 (Albery).

IV

THE AUTHENTIC VICTORIAN

There is no such person, it is often asserted, as the average
man. The human personality and the vicissitudes of life
are so complex and unpredictable that to generalise about
people is to invite criticism that will tend to undermine
the validity of the author's theme. To particularise in
terms of an individual's approximation to the popular
image of a contemporary or historical typology may
also expose the author to the shafts of his critics. Yet,
if I had been asked to describe a prosperous Victorian
man of business in a small country town, I am confident
that the personality that would have emerged would have
borne an uncannily close resemblance to the man revealed
in the pages of Henry Michell's diary. We must ask, therefore, whether it represents the man as he was and would
have been understood by his contemporaries or, as he
saw himself and wished his family to remember him. All
diaries are retrospective; most are written subjectively;
especially those, that like Henry Michell's, are compiled
later in life. I have naturally pondered on this aspect
of the analysis as it is crucial to the value of what he has
to say, and the usefulness of the edited diary to those
who look to it as a contribution to the history of Horsham
in the 19th century.

The problem admits of no conclusive answer. We are
bound to say that we do not know with certainty. However, as far as the evidence goes and judgement permits,
I am satisfied that, except in a marginal sense, we can

generally rely on the facts as stated and the authenticity of the character that is portrayed. The diary is unadorned with other than pardonable flashes of self-satisfaction and there is clearly no spurious attempt to present the diarist in a flattering role. Stylistically, the diary exhibits the serious but relatively uncontrived efforts of a man to whom example, characteristically as a genuine Victorian, was important in the difficult art of bring up a family. In stating, as he did, at the beginning of the diary that it was intended for the family archives, Henry Michell was sincere. It is not the product of a mind anticipating a public interest in his career or political opinions. If it had any other dimensions they were the satisfactions that Henry Michell clearly derived from recording the progress of his business investments and the recollection of exciting and memorable travel.

As a work of modest literary pretensions the diary is interesting rather than impressive. Henry Michell was concerned to inform and instruct his family about the virtues of industry, competence and the careful management of financial affairs. The pleasures of family life are seen as the valued rewards of a successful business career. Although, as a man of substance in Victorian Horsham, he could not but participate in public life and indeed held some vigorous political views, that aspect of his life does not emerge with the same relish as the mounting score of his investments or the strength of his family ties. It was not, indeed, the most significant area of his endeavours. Business he found more rewarding; family life more satisfying. He never entirely reconciled himself to a political role and could not find one with which he was wholly compatible. His energies were devoted to more tangible and less ephemeral objects. We are inevitably disappointed therefore when we look to the diary for an insight into the local political tissue of Horsham society in his time. Henry Michell's concentration on the larger issues with which he was more deeply interested, but not seriously involved, such as the Corn Laws and the Franco-Prussian war emphasises his marginal instincts for local politics. He may be found, on account of his local status, supporting the candidature of parliamentary aspirants, taking the chair and making the occasional speech. His influence was never, it would seem, seriously and continuously exerted in the development of local institutions or even in the formation of opinion. This he reserved for the commercial life of the town in which his place was significant as a creator of well-run and profitable enterprises that were important elements in the local economy. The speculative episode in which he purchased the County Gaol and his prominence in the brewing trade of the area underline Henry Michell's position in business life. 'Henry Michell the Brewer' he has been called; as such he wisely laid the foundations of his commercial success.

'Of all the trades in the world', it was written in 1621, 'a brewer is the loadstone which draws the customers of all functions to it. It is the mark or upshot of every man's ayme, and the bottomless whirlepoole that swallows up the profits of rich and poore. The brewer's art (like a wild kestrel) flies at all games; or like a butler's boxe at Christmasse, it is sure to winne, whosoever loses'. Henry Michell, the brewer of Horsham could have testified to that!

We cannot, therefore, perceive Henry Michell as a politically creative or catalytic figure in Horsham's Victorian period. He was there, on the stage, in the identifiable public posture of a 'big' and affluent man in local terms. His name was associated with local events and local causes and it is as a part of the social fabric of middle-class life in the town that we see him in retrospect. It was people like Henry Michell, all over the country, who, collectively made a major contribution to the stability of family life and the underlying strength of the national economy. It was wealth and jobs, rather than ideas and change, that his efforts generated. In that his

ambitions were of the middle class that enjoyed but did
not aspire to political influence. People like Henry Michell
cared about standards and sought moral, even if sometimes superficial, values. They set too the tone of Victorian England. The flavour of life in Victorian Horsham
owed much to Henry Michell and the rest of the entrepreneurial class to which he belonged. He was, as I am
sure he would have wished to be judged, an authentic
Victorian.

NOTES ON THE TEXT

1. Thomas Creevey: A whig politician and follower of Fox, he was M.P. for Thetford and a member of the ministry of 'All the Talents' in 1806. His journals were published as the Creevey Papers in 1903.

2. Edwin Chadwick: Benthamite secretary of the Poor Law Commission who, in 1842, was responsible for a significant social document in presenting his report on 'The Sanitary Condition of the Labouring Population'.

3. The County Gaol: There have been several main gaols in Horsham, all, as far as is known, in the area of the Carfax and North Street until that built in 1775-9. Previously there had no doubt been local 'lock-ups' and there was a House of Correction on the London road. In earlier times the judicial authorities would have relied on the franchise prisons and, like those in Surrey, even the London gaols. The first gaol for which there is documentary evidence appears to have been built in North Street between 1531 and 1540. This was replaced on the site by the north-east corner of the Carfax about 1600. The third, on the north side of the Carfax was constructed about 1640. It was that building which attracted John Howard's criticism on the grounds that it was 'filthy and unsafe'. The gaol that Henry Michell purchased and demolished was approved by John Howard as 'clean, healthy and well regulated' and stood just north of Queen Street, in a field called Causey (Causeway) Croft, in a position that is now straddled by the railway line. Its future was settled by the decision to transfer the Horsham Assizes to Lewes in 1830, an issue that had arisen as long before as the 16th century when Lewes had been regarded as the more convenient location. It was a matter of some local pride and not without social and economic significance as the Assizes had been

held at Horsham over a period of some 500 years. By 1845, when it was put up for auction the gaol was redundant.

4. Grandford House: The Michell residence that stood behind the Carfax on the north side.

5. Francis Moore: Henry Michell's reference is to the founder of the 'Almanack Improved or the Farmer's and Countryman's Calendar'; its modern version still has its adherents. Such almanacs were, in Henry Michell's time, popular and useful. Moore's was published by the Company of Stationers who also sponsored the county almanacs—Sussex and Surrey were issued in one volume—and others such as the Clerical Almanac and the Goldsmith's Almanac.

6. Sarai (*sic*) Ellis.

7. The Shelley Family: the Michells, who had owned 'ffelde place' (Field Place at Broadbridge Heath) since at least 1524 when it was mentioned in Richard Mychell's will, were closely linked with the Shelleys through marriage. In 1664 Timothy Shelley married Katherine Michell at Horsham. The connection with the poet Percy Bysshe Shelley arose from the marriage in 1751 of Mary Catherine Michell, daughter of the Rev. Theobald Michell of Horsham, with Sir Bysshe Shelley; they were the poet's grandparents. Field Place passed to the Shelleys from the Michells in 1729 when Edward Shelley, whose Michell ancestors had owned it, purchased the property from Ann (Mrs. Slyford) the heiress of John Michell. John Michell had been married to Sir Timothy Shelley's widow, Mary in 1669, a further complication in the genealogical entanglement of the two families over almost 200 years. The diary contains references to Sir Timothy Shelley, father of the poet and son of Mary Catherine Michell, with whom Henry Michell was involved over the brewery property.

8. The Clifton Suspension Bridge: The fine bridge at Clifton, near Bristol, is typical of the achievements of the Victorian engineers. It was designed by Isambard Kingdom Brunel to span the Avon Gorge. Work on the bridge commenced in 1831. Owing to financial difficulties it was not completed until 1864 some five years after its designer's death.

9. The Great Briton: Michell's reference is to the SS *Great Britain* which has, on account of the dramatic story of its recovery from a beach in the Falkland Isles and return to Bristol in 1970, aroused recent topical interest. In Henry Michell's day it, like Brunel's other ships, the *Great Western* and the *Great Eastern,* ranked as one of the heralds of the new steamship age, which was of great significance in the establishment of Britain's maritime supremacy. The *Great Britain* was, in fact, the first iron-hulled screw-driven ship on the high seas. Its adventurous career began in 1843. It was rightly regarded as a milestone in marine engineering.

10. Vaccination: By Henry Michell's time vaccination had begun to establish its prophylactic role in medicine. The technique had been discovered and developed by an English country doctor, Edward Jenner, who published his thesis in 1798-1800. It was first used successfully against smallpox and Jenner's methods were not significantly changed for 100 years.

11. The Ruskins: John Ruskin and his brilliant wife Euphemia both had a considerable influence on literary and artistic taste in Victorian England. Something of a prodigy, Ruskin became a writer and critic of international status.

12. Mona Wilson: in her contribution to 'Early Victorian England' (1934).

13. Kithurst Hill: Henry Michell was incorrect.. This is not the highest point on the Downs west of Chanctonbury. The altitude at Kithurst Hill is 700ft. There are a number of points above 800ft. to the west of this eminence.

14. 'healed in': in Sussex dialect a house is said to be healed (roofed). The word is derived from the Anglo-Saxon word meaning 'to cover'. It can be applied to tiles, slate, or indeed any roofing material, but is commonly taken to refer to the use of Horsham slab and is, therefore, most frequently met in the mid-Sussex context.

15. Abergavenny: The Earls of Abergavenny have for many centuries numbered among the principal families and

landowners of Sussex. The family seat is at Eridge and most of their estates were in East Sussex. In West Sussex the family held the manors of West Chiltington and Nutbourne from the 16th century. Most of the latter property was enfranchised in the 1920s.

16.   The Horsham Permanent Benefit Building Society.

17.   'swipes': literally waste beer.

18.   Gas lighting: The use of gas as an illuminant was discovered by the Chinese at least 2,000 years ago. Natural gas was first produced in Britain in Lancashire in 1664. In Europe gas lighting was introduced in France in 1784. The first practical application of this technique in Britain was by William Murdoch in 1792 in Redruth, Cornwall. It came to London in 1807 and by about 1900 was in general use. The first gas lighting in Horsham dated from 1836.

19.   Water Supplies: Water has been piped to community settlements from early times. Treated and purified supplies in scale date from 1829 when James Simpson constructed a filtration plant to tap the Thames water for London. The importance of this process for hygiene and the prevention of disease led to the large-scale establishment of water utilities in the Victorian era. The Horsham Water Works Company with which Henry Michell was connected as an investor was typical of the private enterprise undertakings of the time. Since then there has been a continuing trend towards bringing these companies into public ownerhip.

20.   Mash vat (or Tun): This was a large vessel, usually of cast iron, in which the mash (crushed malt grain and hot liquor) was treated to separate the liquid malt (wort) from the grist (milled malt grains).

21.   The Gay Street Malthouse: This malthouse (at Colliers' Farm) was associated with a tax scandal of unusual proportions. Over a period of some years the Allen brothers, Alfred, who managed the Horsham malthouse, and Dennett, who operated at Gay Street (West Chiltington) contrived to defraud the Inland Revenue of large sums. By failing to declare hidden stocks of malt,

which therefore escaped duty, they were able to under-
cut their competitors as well as to pay higher prices
to local farmers for the barley crops. Eventually they
were detected when the Revenue Officers, information
having been laid against the Allens, raided the malthouses at Gay Street and elsewhere. The Allens escaped
to America though their malt was confiscated. For
their flagrant offences they were fined £375,000 in
absentia. Later, this was reduced to £110,000 but, in
the end, the Allens were able to return to England on
payment of £10,000.

22. St. Leonard's Fair: There were a number of traditional
fairs in Horsham. The largest was the July Fair which
lasted from at least the early 13th century until its
abolition in 1886. The St. Leonard's Fair was invariably
held on the Common on 17 November near what is now
St. Leonard's Road. In 1813 after the enclosure of the
Common it had to be moved to another site on private
land east of the town. These fairs, apart from their
prime market function were social events in their own
right and the occasion of much merry-making and
excitement in the country towns where they were
held. By the latter half of the 19th century they were
in decline though there are vestiges still in the Bank
Holiday fun fairs of today.

23. The Anti-Corn Law League: The taxation of corn and
other primary produce has been the subject of inter-
mittent political and social controversy from time
immemorial. When, in the early 19th century economic
conditions raised the issue again it became a matter of
cardinal political importance. The League was founded
in 1838 and operated from its headquarters in Man-
chester. It undoubtedly played a leading role in the
campaign for total repeal of the laws governing the
taxes. Although largely a middle-class organisation it
enjoyed, as a result of successful propaganda, wide-
spread support among the labouring community. In the
end it was successful; and it split the Conservative party
in the process when Sir Robert Peel became convinced
of the necessity for repeal.

24. Richard Cobden: He was one of the founders of the

Anti-Corn Law League and an outstanding radical thinker. He was born at Heyshott, near Midhurst in West Sussex, and attended the Grammar School there. In politics his name is linked with John Bright's with whom he co-operated on major political issues.

25. The Great Exhibition: The exhibition of 1851 was the brainchild of Prince Albert and the nation's gesture to the Victorian achievement. It was repeated in a lower key in 1862. Its fascination captivated numerous Victorian families, like that of Henry Michell, who visited the exhibition on several occasions. He never tired of its delights. As a focus of public attention and a royal spectacle it has assumed a symbolic status in the Prince Consort's life. At first sited in Hyde Park it was later moved to Crystal Palace. Paxton's great glass structure was eventually destroyed by fire, but the name has survived.

26. Stanley and Livingstone: David Livingstone's lonely martyrdom in 'Darkest Africa' was the poignant climax in that Victorian hero's life. His exploits thrilled the nation and when he had been missing in Africa since he set out in 1865 a search was demanded. Livingstone had been exploring the Central African lakes and the source (as he believed) of the Nile. The *New York Herald* commissioned the explorer, H. M. Stanley, who found Livingstone at Ujiji, the centre of the Arab slave trade, in November 1871. Despite Stanley's pressure Livingstone refused to return and died by the lakes in April 1873.

27. Edward B. Pusey (1800-1882): Pusey was the leader of the Oxford Movement. The son of a Protestant refugee from Europe he assumed his anglicised name after inheriting property of that name in Berkshire. Whilst at Oriel College, Oxford, he formed an association with J. H. Newman. Pusey was schooled as an orientalist but became interested in theology. Influential tracts upon fasting, baptism and other rites were the product of his brilliant intellect. Though he was always a convinced Anglican he was also leader of the Catholic revival in the Church of England.

28. John Fisher Hodgson, M.A.: Vicar of Horsham from
    1840 to 1883. During his incumbency the parish church
    of St. Mary's was restored, in 1864-5, under the super-
    vision of the architect S. S. Teulon. Like Henry Michell's
    demolition of the gaol it was something of a public
    spectacle in the town.

29. Burrells: The Burrell family were descended from the
    Devon family of Randolphus de Burrell. They were in
    Sussex by the mid-15th century and still live at Knepp
    Castle a few miles south of Horsham. The estate in
    Shipley came into their hands in 1789 through the
    marriage of the antiquary, Sir William Burrell, with
    Sophia Raymond, a wealthy Essex heiress. The ruined
    Norman keep of Knepp Castle is a familiar local land-
    mark. The house, built by John Nash in 1809, was
    destroyed by fire in 1904, but subsequently restored in
    its original form.

30. Gorings: The Goring family, who possess the estates
    at Wiston, near Steyning, have been ensconced there
    for more than 200 years. Wiston House was built for
    Sir Robert Shirley in 1576. It passed to the Gorings
    through marriage in 1743. Sir Charles Goring is remem-
    bered for plantting Chanctonbury Ring in about 1760.

31. Education Act: The Act of 1870 was piloted by W. E.
    Forster whose name is now attached to it. This impor-
    tant legislation marked the advent of universal compul-
    sory education and thus changed the whole course of
    educational development and the concept of social
    responsibility for it.

INDEX